Teaching World Languages
for Specific Purposes

TEACHING WORLD LANGUAGES FOR SPECIFIC PURPOSES

A Practical Guide

Diana M. Ruggiero

Georgetown University Press
Washington, DC

Library of Congress Cataloging-in-Publication Data
Names: Ruggiero, Diana M., author.
Title: Teaching world languages for specific purposes : a practical guide / Diana M. Ruggiero.
Description: Washington, DC : Georgetown University Press, 2022. | Includes bibliographical references and index.
Identifiers: LCCN 2021006586 | ISBN 9781647121587 (hardcover) | ISBN 9781647121594 (paperback) | ISBN 9781647121600 (ebook)
Subjects: LCSH: Languages, Modern—Study and teaching. | Languages, Modern—Study and teaching—Curricula. | Sublanguage—Study and teaching. | Sublanguage—Study and teaching—Curricula.
Classification: LCC PB36 .R84 2022 | DDC 418.0071—dc23
LC record available at https://lccn.loc.gov/2021006586

♾ This paper meets the requirements of ANSI/NISO Z39.48-1992 (Permanence of Paper).

23 22   9 8 7 6 5 4 3 2
First printing

Printed in the United States of America

Cover design by Brad Norr, Hugo, MN
Interior design by Robert Kern, TIPS Publishing Services, Carrboro, NC

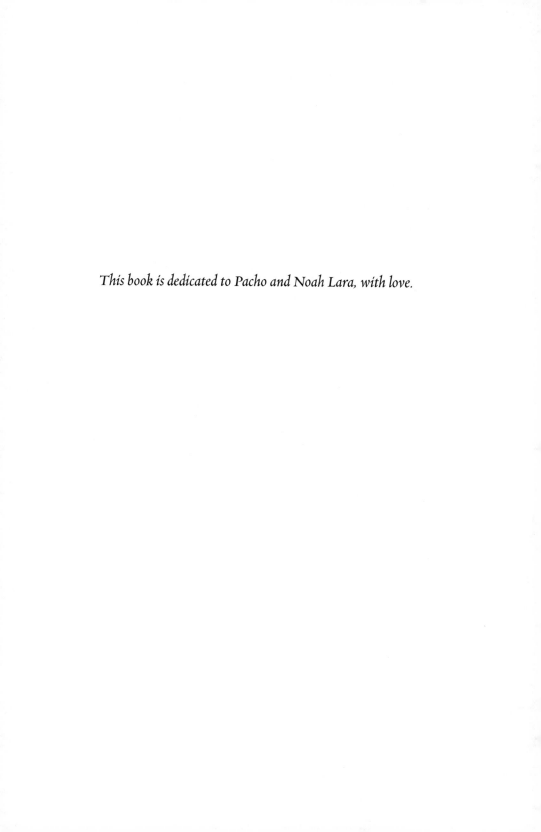

This book is dedicated to Pacho and Noah Lara, with love.

Contents

Preface

THIS BOOK INVITES WORLD language educators of all disciplinary backgrounds and language areas to take up and develop curricula in world languages for specific purposes (WLSP). It is based on over ten years of experience developing coursework in and researching Spanish for specific purposes (SSP), WLSP, and community service learning (CSL) at the postsecondary level. Though other traditions and trajectories of WLSP exist around the world, this book is written from my current vantage point as a faculty member sitting at an institution of higher learning in the United States. That said, the broader concerns to which this book speaks regarding the place and value of world language education today are nonetheless relevant for all world language educators, no matter where they may teach. This has been made that much more apparent in the wake of COVID-19 and the use of social distancing as a public health intervention.

We live in a divided world, even as the world gets smaller; we are increasingly separated by our ever-expanding technology, political and religious ideologies and rhetoric, social identities, national boundaries, and areas of specialization, whether in the workplace, at home, or at our educational institutions. Time and again we are challenged to rise above these divisions and recognize our common humanity to achieve something greater than we can possibly imagine, whether in the context of a pandemic, rampant racial injustices and civil rights abuses, xenophobia, war, natural disasters, or a crisis of the heart. As witnessed over the past century and more recently in the wake of COVID-19 and the global protests over racial injustice and civil rights abuses, society is beginning to awaken to the potential of a new reality, one which values, priorities, and puts into practice core principles of empathy, compassion, and love. What this demands of our educational system is a new approach that likewise foregrounds these values. In the context of world languages education, this means centering and practicing empathy and compassion in how we teach, value, and purpose world languages so as to make it relevant and meaningful in the context of present-day challenges and opportunities. This is where WLSP stands to make a significant contribution.

An interdisciplinary field, WLSP encompasses and yet transcends language acquisition and use for specialized purposes, including the professions and the community. The field originated during the mid-twentieth century at various times and geophysical locations around the globe in order to meet the demands and needs of an emerging global market economy. Business languages and lexical concerns marked its early formation and trajectory within world language education, and within institutions of higher education in the United States, its research and teaching remained the domain largely of applied linguists. Since the mid- to late 1990s and over the course of the past twenty years, however, the field has grown significantly in its scope and objectives and has transcended the research and teaching concerns of its formative years. A major impetus for this transformation has been the shift in the needs of today's economy, educational institutions, world language programs, students, and local communities.

We are moving toward a more socially conscious way of teaching across the curriculum, but especially within world language programs. Gone are the days when we can solely concern ourselves with teaching students how to order food at a restaurant or find their way to the library or the bathroom in the target language. Rather, we have shifted our objectives to meet the demands of our students, programs, employers, and the community. For world languages, this means moving away from a concern with lexicon to a desire to foster and facilitate effective communication within specific contexts. As a result, cultural knowledge, intercultural sensitivity and competence, intercultural communication, and community engagement are now at the center of world language higher education. This book is written from and presents the teaching of WLSP from this current perspective in world language higher education.

In writing this book, my purpose is to create a better world for and through my students and the work that I do as a world language educator teaching WLSP in higher education. I began teaching Spanish as a way to share with students my cultural heritage, background, and experiences as an Argentine and Latinx woman living in the United States, as well as my love of language learning and the diverse cultures of the Spanish-speaking world. Over the years, and as a result of my teaching experiences at three different institutions of higher education, I transitioned from teaching core curriculum courses in languages and culture to teaching Spanish for specific purposes and the community. With a background in cultural studies, and having taken and later taught an influential course in Spanish for the communities as a graduate student at The Ohio State University, I began to develop curricula and research in the teaching of WLSP that spoke to my strengths as a teacher and that reflected my background, interests, and values as a scholar and socially conscious individual. My student-centered approach to education led me to develop a teaching and research agenda that focused largely on languages, cultures, and communities, with an eye toward developing student intercultural sensitivity and competence. To this end, I integrated culture and community service learning into my teaching of WLSP and focused on empowering my students to find their purpose in learning and using language as a vehicle for social change. This perspective is reflected in the teaching strategies, sample teaching materials, and resources presented in this book.

Despite the call for a more expansive and responsive curriculum in world language higher education and the subsequent growth of WLSP at the K–12 and undergraduate level, I find myself still at the edge of a field that is largely marginalized within many graduate-level programs in world languages. As a field well positioned to deliver the objectives of the Modern Language Association (MLA), as stated in their 2007 call for change, WLSP is the future of world language higher education in the twenty-first century. The continued growth of the field is now up to our students, and if we are not preparing them to teach what today's and tomorrow's students, institutions, employers, and society want, need, and demand, then we are closing the door on an opportunity to make a significant and meaningful contribution to the modern world. Alongside my colleagues in WLSP, it is my objective, through my research, courses, and this book, to help bring WLSP to the forefront of the higher education and the graduate world-language curriculum.

As a heuristic model, this book demonstrates a way of thinking about WLSP curriculum development that goes beyond cookie-cutter lesson plans and activities. The goal is to empower individual teachers to build their own WLSP courses, lesson plans, and teaching materials based on their respective strengths, backgrounds, needs, and creativity; keeping in focus those of their students, institutions, and local communities. Though specialized language skills and preprofessional training will always remain central to WLSP, they are resourced here in service to the formation of empathic, compassionate, and mindful students and future leaders in the professions and the community. Such a socially conscious perspective in the teaching of WLSP and world language education is not only timely and relevant as an educational trend in helping our students succeed professionally, but a necessity for making our world a better place for all.

Organization of Chapters

Drawing on my own research and teaching experience, this book consists of twelve chapters divided into three major sections, suggested print and online resources, and an appendix. The content encompasses foundations, curriculum development, and teaching strategies and addresses issues, challenges, models, and resources in the teaching of WLSP. Though based on my graduate-level WLSP course in the area of SSP, it is written in English and speaks broadly to the teaching of WLSP. As such, scholars, educators, and students in other languages will find this book useful for their own courses in WLSP pedagogy, or as a resource in developing their own curricula in WLSP teaching. In this way, I hope to reach a broader audience and to spark a translingual discussion on the topic among world language educators and students.

Chapters 1 through 3, the first major section, provide relevant contextual and background information as well as resources for teaching WLSP. Specifically, chapter 1 offers key definitions and addresses core concepts and issues regarding the scope and aims of WLSP. Drawing on existing research, chapter 2 briefly outlines the known benefits of WLSP and further addresses the place and relevance of WLSP in higher education. Lastly, chapter 3 provides practical solutions and resources for teachers and students preparing to teach in WLSP.

Chapters 4 through 6, the second major section, consider in greater detail core aspects of WLSP curriculum development. Chapter 5 covers WLSP course design (i.e., syllabi, lesson planning, activities, assessments) while chapters 6 and 7 address community engagement and CSL project design in WLSP, respectively. Issues, challenges, and practical strategies and models are addressed in each chapter.

Chapters 8 through 11, the third major section, present teaching strategies, models, and exercises for specific challenges in WLSP pedagogy. Chapter 7 shows teachers and students how to integrate WLSP into non-WLSP specific courses, providing sample lesson plans and activities. Chapter 8 similarly demonstrates how teachers might approach interpreting in the WLSP classroom and lesson. How to incorporate culture in WLSP is addressed in chapter 9, while the needs of heritage language learners are discussed in chapter 10. In the wake of COVID-19, chapter 11 presents ways in which communication technology can be used to bridge teaching and community engagement challenges posed by such extreme measures as social distancing, highlighting the relevance of WLSP for education and society in the process.

Lastly, the appendixes present selected print and online resources as well as sample teaching materials and activities. Though drawn from my teaching experience in the area of SSP and far from comprehensive, the list of sources contained in the appendixes are nonetheless useful as a starting point for further developing curricula in WLSP and are intended to be broadly applicable to all world languages taught at the postsecondary level. Among the items included in the appendix are models of course syllabi and calendars, assignments, assessments, and learning activities. The appendix materials are likewise meant to be heuristic and therefore applicable across any language area. Teachers are encouraged to use them as a basis for developing their own curriculum materials. It is my hope that teachers, regardless of their background, find and contribute their own respective voice and strengths as a world language educator to the teaching of WLSP.

Acknowledgments

I AM GRATEFUL TO numerous scholars in the world of WLSP for their mentorship, collaboration, and friendship. Among them, I would like to thank Sheri Spaine Long, Anne Abbott, Lourdes Sánchez-López, Barbara Lafford, Carmen King de Ramirez, Mary Long, Mary Risner, Darcy Lear, Mary Long, Ethel Jorge, Michael Doyle, Josef Hellebrandt, Glenn Martinez, and Francisco Salgado for believing in me, taking me under their wing, working alongside me, and helping me to become the scholar and professional that I am today. In addition, I am most thankful for the continued support of my colleagues around the world that make up the American Association of Teachers of Spanish and Portuguese (AATSP), American Council on the Teaching of Foreign Languages (ACTFL), and the Modern Language Association (MLA).

I am also grateful to several colleagues both in and outside of world language higher education for their continued friendship and moral support over the years. I am particularly grateful to John Maddox, Christina Garcia, Elizabeth Pettinaroli, Eric Henager, Timothy Gaster, Claudia Fernández, Chita Espina-Bravo, and Sergio Troitiño. Their collaboration, perspective, and mentorship has been invaluable to my formation as a scholar and person.

At the University of Memphis, my home institution, I am most thankful for the support of my colleagues in the Department of World Languages and Literatures and the College of Arts and Sciences (CAS). Among them, I am particularly grateful for the support of Thomas Nenon, dean of CAS, my chair, William Thompson, and my departmental colleagues and friends Ralph Albanese, Fernando Burgos, Fatima Nogueira, Francisco Vivar, Pilar Alcalde, Monika Nenon, Glynda Luttman, and Patricia Pinkey. I am also grateful for the support of my colleagues around campus that make up the Engaged Scholarship Committee. In particular, I am thankful to the University of Memphis and the Engaged Scholarship Committee for a 2015 Community Engagement Capacity Building Grant and to my department and the CAS for awarding me funds for research and travel toward my professional development and the completion of this book. I am particularly grateful for the friendship and mentorship of Katherine Lambert-Pennington, Charles Santo, Richard Lou,

Balaji Krishnan, and Zabihollah Rezaee. My success would not have been possible without the support of my University colleagues, the administration, and staff.

In addition, my work in engaged scholarship and CSL would not be possible without the support and collaboration of my community partners. I am especially grateful to Ohni Johns, founder and former director of Caritas Village, for her friendship and assistance with the Creating Communities, Engaged Scholarship (CruCES) service-learning project. Thank you also to Richard Lou, founder and former director of the Centro Cultural Latino de Memphis for his assistance in that same project. I am also thankful for the support and collaboration of Giovana Lopez and CazaTeatro, Mauricio Calvo and Latino Memphis, Church Health, and the YMCA of Cordova.

I reserve a special place in my heart for my students, both undergraduate and graduate, over the years. Thank you in particular to Rosa Mena, who helped research and compile the list of suggested print and online resources in this book. I am also grateful to my students in SPAN 7895 (Teaching Spanish for Specific Purposes and Civic Engagement), SPAN 4703 (Spanish for Community Engagement), SPAN 4704 (Spanish for Health Care), SPAN 4793 (Medical Interpreting and Translating), and SPAN 4702 and 4701 (Spanish for Commerce 1 and 2) for providing support for my research in WLSP pedagogy and for feedback on this book. I would also like to thank my graduate assistants for their support as well.

As a graduate student at The Ohio State University, I took and later taught a course titled Spanish in Ohio that would mark the beginning of my interest in WLSP and CSL and the teaching of WLSP from a socially conscious perspective. I am grateful to Terrell Morgan for introducing me to this "other" way of teaching languages as well as for his friendship and mentorship over the years. A special thank you also to Jan Macian, then language coordinator at OSU, for helping me to discover my love of teaching Spanish so many years ago. They were both there to support me, lift me up, and encourage me when I was uncertain of whether I had the background and qualifications to teach that which my heart was compelling me to pursue and to do it in the way that I knew was right. I am also grateful to my other mentors and friends at The Ohio State University, including Jan Macian, Lúcia Costigan, and Ileana Rodríguez, among others, who have likewise influenced my formation as an educator, believed in me as a scholar, and supported me over the years.

A special thank you to Hope LeGro, the reviewers of this book, and the editorial board and staff at Georgetown University Press for believing in me and helping bring this book to fruition. And last but not least, I would not have been able to complete this labor of love if not for the support also of my family and friends, specifically Francisco and Noah Lara, Leo and Kathy Lara, the Lara clan, my family in Argentina, the Ruggiero family, and my friends in Columbus, Ohio, Monmouth, Illinois, and Memphis, Tennessee. To anyone I may have left out unintentionally and to the readers of this book, I thank you for your support.

1

Teaching WLSP

THIS BOOK IS ABOUT the teaching of world languages for specific purposes (WLSP) and its place and value within the landscape of higher education. Based on over ten years of curriculum development, teaching, and research experience in the field of WLSP as well as on current best practices in the field, it provides postsecondary world language educators of all language teaching and educational backgrounds with practical strategies, teaching examples and materials, and resources for developing courses, lessons, and assignments in WLSP and in community-service learning (CSL), a key learning tool connecting the classroom and community in the teaching of WLSP. Though perhaps unfamiliar territory for world language educators with backgrounds in literature and culture, the teaching of WLSP encompasses and accommodates a diverse range of pedagogical methods. World language teachers of all backgrounds already possessing a foundation in world language pedagogy will therefore find this book useful as a complement to their existing curricula and approach to language teaching. The strategies, examples, and resources presented here are therefore offered as a launching point for professional development and as a heuristic guide in the teaching of WLSP.

The world today is changing, and language departments at institutions of higher learning around the world are rethinking and revamping their vision and curricular offerings as a result. WLSP presents a solution to these challenges in that it reflects a move toward bridging the classroom and community, the student and the workplace, and language, culture, and society through the study of language and culture in specific contexts. As a means of providing teachers and students with contextual and background information on WLSP and the contents of this book, this chapter introduces the field of WLSP, its definition, scope, and objectives, and briefly addresses how this book can serve as a resource in the development and teaching of WLSP curricula in higher education.

WLSP: Definition, Aim and Scope
For the purposes of this book, WLSP is defined as an interdisciplinary, multidisciplinary, and transdisciplinary field encompassing the teaching, learning, and research

of languages within and for specific, purpose driven contexts (Ruggiero 2019a, 49). This includes the professions, community initiatives, community uses for and by language users, and the arts. WLSP is interdisciplinary and multidisciplinary in that it is informed by and contributes to many different related disciplines and fields, such as linguistics and cultural studies, and transdisciplinary in that it transcends the boundaries of any one specific discipline or field.

The term WLSP was first proposed by Barbara Lafford, Carmen King de Ramírez, and the contributing authors of the edited volume *Transferable Skills for the 21st Century* with the publication of that same volume (King de Ramírez and Lafford 2018, 4). Its use is intended to differentiate WLSP from the related field of English Language for Specific Purposes, also referred to as ESP, ELSP, and LSP, with respect to its divergent research and teaching aims and objectives, including its focus on world languages, cultures, and communities. Among the primary concerns of this group of scholars was the idea that WLSP has more to contribute to students, language programs, and the world than specialized language skills. Though indeed important, it is not understood as the sole objective of WLSP pedagogy.

With the growth in scholarship in and relating to WLSP, there have been a number of definitions of the field offered, whether implicitly or explicitly (see Ruggiero 2019a). Many of these definitions depart from the traditional view of WLSP as commerce-centered and language-acquisition-focused to recognize the interdisciplinary nature of the field and to include other specific contexts and pedagogical objectives, such as the community and intercultural and translingual competence (e.g., Doyle 2018; King de Ramírez and Lafford 2018; M. Long 2017b; Sánchez-López 2013a). This trend in the emerging scholarship reflects the recent shift in world language education currently envisioned by the Modern Language Association (see MLA 2007) and the current institutional, departmental, student, and community needs and demands observed in the United States in particular (M. Long 2017a, 1). This book, in its definition of the field and in its pedagogical orientation, reflects this trend and contributes to existing definitions in recognizing its transdisciplinary nature.

The teaching of WLSP, such as for health care, commerce, and the community, is relatively new in the history of world language education. Most scholars place the origins of this movement globally in the mid-twentieth century, following the second world war (M. Long 2017a, 2). By all accounts, the initial emphasis worldwide was on language for business and on the need to provide students with the necessary language skills to successfully compete in the emerging modern global market economy (see Grosse and Voght 1990; King de Ramírez and Lafford 2018; M. Long 2017b). Since that time, however, this diverse field has grown significantly in its pedagogical objectives and scope as well as in its research agenda, matching the distinct and shifting needs and demands of higher education, language departments, students, the market economy, national interests, and local communities (see M. Long 2017b; Sánchez-López, Long, and Lafford 2017). Today, WLSP is a fast growing field of research and teaching distinct in its aim and scope that is coming into its own in the twenty-first century (Lafford 2012; M. Long 2017b; Ruggiero 2018c; Sánchez-López, Long, and Lafford 2017).[1]

Courses in WLSP to date span the professions, the arts, community initiatives, and community uses for and by language users. These include courses in language for commerce, health care, the legal professions and law enforcement, public services, translation and interpreting, and broader courses exploring the intersection of language and culture within specific contexts in local communities, among others. Courses in WLSP often integrate community-based education and outreach initiatives, such as internships, service learning, and community-centered courses. In linking language, culture, and community, WLSP is well positioned to fulfill the Five C's of the American Council on the Teaching of Foreign Languages (ACTFL) World Readiness Standards: communication, cultures, connections, comparisons, and communities (Abbott and Lear 2010). These are the foundations upon which language programs are now building their curricula and other initiatives. Though community-based education is sporadically used across the world language curriculum, it is a central component of WLSP (see Ruggiero 2018b).

Current research in WLSP reflects these concerns and increases in interest in the field. Over the past twenty years, numerous conference panels, national and international conferences, and organizations on WLSP have emerged as well as scholarly articles and special journal issues on WLSP as well as on community service learning (CSL), including focus issues of the periodicals *Hispania* and the *Modern Language Journal* (Sánchez-López, Long, and Lafford 2017, 13; Ruggiero 2018b). New peer-reviewed journals devoted specifically to WLSP have also surfaced, as have edited volumes, including the periodicals *Journal of Languages for Specific Purposes*, *Business Languages*, and volumes edited by Mary Long (2017), Lourdes Sánchez-López (2013c), and Carmen King de Ramírez and Barbara Lafford (2018). More recently, teaching materials such as textbooks, manuals, and method books have also surfaced (e.g., Abbott 2009; Blanca 2012; Lear 2019; Risner n.d.; Trace, Hudson, and Brown 2015). Collectively, the recent scholarship provides readers with a significant overview of the field: its scope and aims, history, and research and teaching objectives and methods.

As the current academic literature on WLSP shows, the aim of WLSP is to produce students who are capable of not only navigating competently within a global economy, but also contributing to the betterment of local communities in meaningful and interculturally competent ways.[2] The question of who is qualified to teach WLSP and how to approach the pedagogy of WLSP, however, is currently being negotiated as the field expands. This book addresses these questions in inviting world language educators of all backgrounds to participate in the development of this emerging field.

Teaching WLSP

Currently, WLSP does not represent a new pedagogical theory or approach in the teaching of world languages. Rather, as a multi-, trans- and interdisciplinary field, it accommodates a broad and diverse range of teaching methodologies currently espoused and used in world language education. What does unite the field with regard to teaching, however, is an emphasis on student-centered learning (M. Long

2017, 4). For this reason, much of the discussion surrounding teaching and learning in WLSP revolves around the question of student, program, and community needs (M. Long 2017a, 4; Sánchez-López 2013a, x). For the purposes of this book, it is therefore more useful to think in terms of student learning needs and common objectives in the teaching of WLSP in higher education.

There are currently three main goals that WLSP teachers, regardless of disciplinary background, strive toward in delivering their courses: (1) teach specialized language and grammar for the benefit of aspiring professionals, (2) teach cultural knowledge for use within specific contexts for ease of cross-cultural communication, and (3) foster intercultural competence for the benefit of individuals and the community (M. Long 2017a, 4; King de Ramírez and Lafford 2018, 2; Ruggiero 2018b). More recently, greater emphasis is being placed on the part of WLSP scholars on social justice and leadership (e.g., Derby et al. 2017; Doyle 2018; S. Long et al. 2014; Martinez 2010; Ruggiero 2018c), cultural awareness and intercultural sensitivity (e.g., King de Ramírez 2016; McBride 2010; Petrov 2013; Ruggiero 2018a, 2019b), the community (e.g., Abbott 2009; Abbott and Dias 2018; Hellebrandt and Varona 1999; Lear and Abbott 2010; Ruggiero 2018c), and transferable skills (see King de Ramirez and Lafford 2018). As a result, it can be said that WLSP pedagogy is concerned with producing well-rounded students who are able to contribute meaningfully not only to their professional workplace, but to their communities and society as a whole.[3]

Following these trends, the strategies, examples, and resources offered in this book reflect the objectives and concerns of WLSP teachers and are in keeping with the current student-centered curricular design emphasis observed in the teaching of WLSP (M. Long 2017a, 4). For this reason, I place particular care in this book to suggest teaching strategies and curricular examples that are student-centered in addition to context-specific and culture- and community-oriented. Among the types of teaching activities and materials I include in this book, for example, are the following:

- Community-based learning activities
- Experiential learning activities
- Metacognitive activities
- Reflective assignments
- Formative assessments
- WLSP syllabi, calendars, and lesson plans
- Cultural activities and strategies for connecting the teaching and learning of WLSP with culture and community

In addition, I include strategies for addressing the following common topics in the teaching of WLSP:

- Student and teacher readiness
- WLSP course design
- Lesson planning for WLSP-specific courses
- Integrating WLSP topics and objectives in non-WLSP courses

- Developing community partnerships for CSL projects in WLSP
- Developing and integrating CSL projects in WLSP
- Teaching interpreting for WLSP
- Integrating culture into WLSP for the purposes of developing intercultural competence
- Teaching WLSP for heritage learners (HLs)
- WLSP in the time of COVID-19

It is important to note that the strategies, sample teaching materials, and resources included in this book are not intended to be comprehensive. Rather, they are intended to serve as a launching point from which to build and grow further in the teaching of WLSP in higher education. Indeed, as best practices and paradigms in world language higher education change with time, this list and the very contents of this book are certain to grow and evolve. I therefore recommend that this book be used alongside existing texts in WLSP research and teaching as well as in world language pedagogy. I also recommend that the suggested strategies and sample course materials provided in this book be taken as a heuristic guide that can be used toward the development of your own curricular materials. How and whether you choose to integrate the suggested strategies and adapt the course materials will depend on your purposes as well as on the circumstances informing your decisions, including but not limited to your needs and those of your students, program, institution, and community as well as the resources available to you.

As world language programs in higher education and institutions of higher learning increasingly emphasize praxis and community engagement in teaching and scholarship, more teachers capable of teaching WLSP will be required. In my years of teaching in higher education, it has become clear to me that WLSP is much more than a topic and subject matter, and it is my hope that this book serves you in developing WLSP curricula for your classroom, department, institution, student body, and community.

Notes

1. For a more thorough overview and critical discussion of definitions of the field, see King de Ramírez and Lafford (2018), M. Long (2017), and Ruggiero (2019a).
2. See, for example, Doyle (2018); King de Ramírez (2017); Lafford, Abbott, and Lear (2014); and Ruggiero (2018a).
3. This much is evident in perusing the respective chapters in the edited volumes on LSP/WLSP pedagogy. See, for example, chapters in King de Ramírez and Lafford (2018), M. Long (2017), and Sánchez-López (2013c).

2

WLSP in Higher Education

THIS CHAPTER IS ABOUT the current place and relevance of WLSP in higher education. In addition to providing historical context, it addresses the overall benefits of WLSP for student language learning and provides a pedagogical foundation for the teaching of WLSP. The current landscape of world language higher education is changing, responding, in part, to shifts in student, market, societal, and institutional needs and priorities. WLSP can be understood as a response or outgrowth of these dynamics, one that seeks to reassert the relevance of world language programs within higher education. As argued in this chapter, the growing demand for WLSP courses and the need to integrate WLSP more fully into the mainstream world language curriculum means greater emphasis in the training and preparation of educators in WLSP at the graduate, PhD program level. It also means further reorienting world language pedagogy toward a more diverse, relevant, and socially responsive curriculum. WLSP is well positioned to make a significant contribution toward this agenda.

WLSP in Postsecondary Education

WLSP is a growing field of research and teaching at the secondary and postsecondary level. Within the United States, its origins are generally situated within the context of the emerging global market economy following the second world war and, later, the subsequent development of business language courses and Centers for International Business Education and Research (CIBER) programs in the United States (see Grosse and Voght 1990; King de Ramírez and Lafford 2018; M. Long 2017b). The initial focus of business language courses and the CIBER programs was in preparing American professionals and businesses for successful competition in the global economy. Given this focus, it is not surprising that the emphasis of many early courses and programs in WLSP was in providing specialized vocabulary and language skills for effective communication (King de Ramírez and Lafford 2018, 2). As a result, the trend in WLSP programs, up until recently, has been a sustained focus, almost exclusively, on business languages and on providing preprofessional language skills, including translation and interpreting (see Grosse and Voght 1990).

Since the late 1990s and early 2000s, the focus of WLSP has expanded beyond a business language and language acquisition focus to other specialized contexts and pedagogical needs and interests. An increasing emphasis in courses, certificate programs, and research in the areas of languages for medicine, for example, have become increasingly popular, as have courses and publications in languages in service to the community (see King de Ramírez and Lafford 2018; Ruggiero 2016, 2018b). Institutions and world language programs at both the secondary and postsecondary level have responded to the changing needs of the global marketplace and of local communities by developing undergraduate minors, certificate programs, and graduate courses in WLSP or specialized areas, such as in medicine. This expansion of the curriculum is reflected in the increasing number of job calls for teachers with specialization in WLSP, as well as the proliferation of publications in WLSP (see Sánchez-López, Long, and Lafford 2017).

The growth of the field has also contributed to a diversity of perspectives in research and teaching. Beyond linguistic concerns, the literature on WLSP shows an increasing interest in providing students with cultural knowledge and opportunities to develop intercultural competence as well as social and leadership skills (see King de Ramírez and Lafford 2018). As the literature on WLSP shows, courses centered on community, pedagogy, heritage learners, education, special needs, and health and wellness, as well as interpreting from a WLSP perspective, are currently of interest to WLSP educators and students. While the overwhelming majority of courses and programs in WLSP are still in the area of the professions and remain on the margins of the world language education at the postsecondary level, there is an evident awareness of the need to integrate WLSP topics and perspectives into the core of the curriculum.

In order to meet the current needs and demands of world language programs, students, and institutions, graduate courses in WLSP and as a part of the core graduate curriculum are necessary. As the field and focus of world language education expands, graduate students will require a broader education and specialized training in the area of WLSP, including its pedagogy. A foreseeable outcome of the current trend in world language higher education and of this awareness may well be the addition of graduate certificates and master's and PhD specializations in WLSP. Regardless, the transformation of world language programs envisioned by the Modern Language Association (2007) is likely only achievable with a more thorough integration of WLSP at the core of graduate-level world language education. This means producing master's and PhD students who can develop curriculum and teach at not only the K–12 level, but at the postsecondary level as well (Ruggiero 2015, 2018b).

Benefits of WLSP for Students and World Language Programs

There are many documented benefits of WLSP for world language programs beyond vocabulary acquisition and grammar. These are discussed at length in many articles and book chapters and one need only peruse one of the many edited volumes and special issues to see the breadth and depth of research into this area and of teaching in WLSP. Suffice it to say that WLSP is known to enhance student language skills, provide preprofessional training, expose students to new career opportunities, and foment lifelong learning skills (M. Long 2017a, 5). As M. Long notes, this is vital to enhancing student life beyond the classroom and beyond their academic careers (M. Long 2017a, 6). It is also important in allowing students the opportunity to engage with the local community beyond classroom study of local issues, policies, and problems toward the resolution of current challenges (e.g., Julseth 2004; Falce-Robinson and Strother 2012; Isabelli and Muse 2016; Martínez 2010; Ruggiero and Hill 2016; Ruggiero 2018a, 2019b; Sánchez-López 2013c). As the recent emphasis on community as an integral part of language learning suggests, providing students with hands-on opportunities to engage with local issues and find meaningful solutions is the key to world language education transformation in the twenty-first century.

While it is true that WLSP is concerned with the acquisition of profession specific vocabulary, it goes well beyond that to inform other areas of language development. As shown in this book, for example, a student learning about medical Spanish will also learn valuable information pertaining to history and culture and sometimes even about literature and general concepts in grammar as well (e.g., Bloom 2008; Martinez 2010; Martinez and Schwartz 2012; Medina and Gordon 2014; Pereira 2015; Zapata 2011). In addition, language conversation, comprehension, and writing skills are also acquired by doing the assignments and the tasks required for the courses (e.g., Llombart-Huesca and Pulido 2007; McBride 2010; Nelson and Scott 2008; Tocaimaza-Hatch and Walls 2016). These reinforce what students are learning in their other language courses and will only help them to grow stronger in these skill areas.

There are other benefits as well. Student motivation for language learning and for engaging with local communities of the target language through the professions may increase as a result of the student- and community-centered focus of WLSP curricula (see M. Long 2010, 2017; Ruggiero 2017c). Similarly, student use of language in profession- and community-specific contexts may increase intercultural competence and student awareness of cultural sensitivity issues, which may lead to greater empathy and compassion among students who will become professionals and community members in intercultural contexts (see McBride 2010; Petrov 2013; Ruggiero 2018a). In today's global economy, cultural knowledge along with language skills are vital to being able to communicate effectively and appropriately in the context of culturally and linguistically diverse workplaces. Indeed, as discussed next, the development of intercultural competence, a major agenda item of the MLA for twenty-first century world language education (see MLA 2007), is one of the primary benefits of WLSP beyond language acquisition cited by scholars in the field (see King de Ramírez and Lafford 2018; M. Long 2017b; and Ruggiero 2018a).

Cultural Awareness and Intercultural Sensitivity and Competence in WLSP Higher Education

In addition to the focus on language development and communicative competence, what WLSP offers students is an opportunity to develop cultural awareness and intercultural sensitivity and competence. Intercultural competence refers to the ability of an individual to behave and communicate "effectively and appropriately" across and move between two or more cultures to achieve a particular objective (see Deardorff 2006, 254; see also Deardorff 2009; Spitzberg and Changnon 2009). This implies awareness of and sensitivity toward issues of relevance in the construction of cultural identity, including those linguistic, social, behavioral, and attitudinal aspects that may factor in intercultural communication (Spitzberg and Changnon 2009, 7; see also Deardorff 2006, 2009). In the case of WLSP, this has translated into the acquisition of specialized language skills, a deepening of cultural knowledge, and a broadening of awareness regarding cultural heterogeneity within the target language. With the addition of CSL, this also means developing intercultural sensitivity, a precursor to intercultural competence, through prolonged exposure to cultural diversity within the community (see Bennett 1993; Ruggiero 2018a). Regardless of course topic or of pedagogical orientation and objective, intercultural competence is central to the teaching of WLSP and is in keeping with the stated objectives of the MLA (2007) and ACTFL.

Related to this and yet absent from discussions of intercultural competence and WLSP is mindfulness in language use. In other words, what words and phrases we choose, when, and how we use them in communication with one another in diverse cultural contexts ought to be a central component of WLSP and world language education in general. This foregrounds cultural awareness and intercultural sensitivity and involves a reflection on empathy and compassion and what it means for world language teachers and students alike. Such a reflection would entail addressing language use not from the perspective of the language itself (i.e., vocabulary, grammar, and spoken and written proficiency), but the intentions behind the use of the language. In terms of teaching, this means focusing on how one chooses to speak to others rather than how one composes a sentence or paragraph or piece of writing. How we treat one another, in other words, ought to be a primary concern of WLSP and world language education, and we need to attend to this level of language use in order to affect change in our student population, in the community at large, and in the world.

Lastly, in attending to intercultural competence in cross-cultural interactions, WLSP and world language education in general needs to attend more closely to nonverbal communication. Nonverbals include extra linguistic aspects of communication, including body language (e.g., facial expressions, gestures, gaze, posture), and sounds that have no lexical meaning (e.g., sighing, laughing, filler words; see Knapp, Hall, and Horgan 2014). A focus on nonverbals is significant in that they can be reflective of the underlying beliefs and attitudes of the users and inform the way in which we begin to interact with others even before we speak or write (Knapp, Hall, and Horgan 2014, 8; see also Ruggiero 2017a). Within WLSP, body language in particular can be easily integrated into lessons focused on interpreting, for example, as shown in this book. Regardless of how nonverbals are integrated, a greater emphasis on this level of communication is necessary in order to fully realize the goal of developing intercultural competence.

In short, we live in a time of much conflict, and cross-cultural relations are at an all time low. In order to change this for the better, we need to preoccupy ourselves with the internal development of our students and not just the external development reflected in the mind and in their behaviors and skills. We need to offer them opportunities to engage with others who are not like them, and in the case of heritage learners, we need to likewise provide them with the opportunity to engage with a diversity of people who may share similar cultural values and the language, but who come from different backgrounds and who may even speak differently from them. WLSP and CSL provide higher education world language programs with the means of making such a transformation for this new century.

3

Teacher and Student Readiness

THIS CHAPTER ADDRESSES TEACHER and student readiness in the development of WLSP curricula. In my experience teaching, researching, and leading curriculum design workshops in the field of WLSP, there are many questions that ought to be considered prior to developing courses and lesson plans in WLSP. Indeed, even before creating a syllabus or lesson plan for a WLSP course, it is only fair to ask whether the appropriate resources exist. For example, what qualifications (i.e., education and professional experience) are necessary to teach a course on world languages for commerce, health care, law enforcement, the community, or other specific purposes? What preparation do students need (language proficiency, educational background, degree or certificate program, professional experience, etc.)? What resources are available to help teachers and students succeed in the WLSP classroom? These questions are often left implicit or are neglected altogether in the current academic literature in WLSP. In my experience, however, asking such questions is important in that the answers will likely factor into the decisions made in the development of WLSP curricula.

To better assist teachers in the preparation of WLSP-focused courses and lessons, the following considers these among other questions informing the curricular design process. In addition, this chapter also considers how the classroom, campus, and community might also be leveraged as resources in the teaching of WLSP. Based on my experience teaching, developing curricula in, and researching WLSP, the contents of this chapter are organized into two main sections that respectively address (1) teacher and student qualifications and preparation, and (2) classroom, campus, and community resources. Building competence and confidence among teachers and students to begin designing WLSP-focused curricula is the primary objective of this chapter.

Assessing Readiness

Context and individual perception play a major role in determining whether one is ready to teach or undertake study in WLSP. Developing a lesson plan in medical

Spanish for a beginner-level Spanish class within a broader unit on the human body requires different preparation needs than an entire course on the same topic for advanced undergraduate and graduate students. That said, in both instances the difference lies more in the attitude and approach of the instructor than in the content of the material itself.

Though certainly beneficial, education, training, and experience in a given area are only part of the bigger picture when it comes to deciding who is and who is not ready to teach or study. Equally if not more important, however, is an individual's level of confidence, motivation, desire, and ability to successfully integrate content knowledge with broader world language learning objectives. For teachers this means recognizing personal strengths and weaknesses in the area of specialization, knowing what resources exist to help close the knowledge gap, and trusting in their ability to apply those resources in ways that appropriately fulfill course objectives. For students specifically this means identifying what knowledge and experience they bring to the classroom (including language proficiency, cultural experience, and professional training), recognizing assumptions and expectations they might be bringing to the class, and maintaining a "beginner's mind" as they progress through the course.

Often, teachers and students bring assumptions and expectations that serve as stumbling blocks. These limiting beliefs are often rooted in fear that stems from a sense of lack, as in the perception of a deficiency in content knowledge. Perhaps the most important lesson of this book speaks directly to this issue, and it is that wherever you as a teacher or student may be in your preparation and training, know that it is enough. As the by now popular adage goes, "You are perfect as you are." Though it may sound cliché, it is most true in this case. Accepting this fact is the first concrete step in not only undertaking WLSP with confidence, but in making it your own. As a teacher or student, this means making it personally and professionally relevant. In other words, make meaningful connections between what you are learning and teaching and what you already know and do as an educator and student. Doing so will only enhance the teaching and learning experience and will also allow for deeper and more meaningful connections and conversations in the classroom.

So, in summary, how do you know if you are qualified to teach or undertake study in WLSP? The answer is surprisingly simple: you are already qualified by virtue of your interest and curiosity. Though this point may be argued by certain specialists, understand that, as noted in chapter 1, WLSP transcends and encompasses a diversity of disciplinary perspectives and is therefore not limited by any one of them. In fact, as a field of teaching and study, WLSP can only be enriched by the inclusion of new and different perspectives and methodologies. What makes you unique as an individual, scholar, and teacher will almost certainly translate to your approach to and teaching of WLSP.

Teacher Preparation

Knowing that you are enough is half the battle in preparing to teach a lesson or course in WLSP. From there, however, you need to assess what strengths you possess and bring as well as recognize the limits of your content knowledge and then bridge the gap. Making newly acquired information meaningful for you and your classroom and students, however, requires an additional step: integrating content knowledge with your existing knowledge and strengths as an educator, professional, and individual. This brings us full circle and highlights the central theme of this book: effective teaching, whether in WLSP, literature, culture, or linguistics, is centered on the way content is integrated, delivered, and processed to serve you, the students, and the communities you collectively serve through your education and training. You are at the center of this process.

Regardless of disciplinary background and training, you bring a unique perspective that will inevitably inform your lesson or class in WLSP in a distinct way. Leverage this as a resource because this is your personal stamp that will differentiate your WLSP course and lesson plan from that of any other teacher at any other institution. Consider the following questions:

- What strengths do I bring as a teacher?
- What educational and professional experience do I bring?
- What other interests, passions, motivations, and expertise do I bring as an individual?
- How might I leverage my personal, educational, and professional background, training, and experience as a resource in my teaching?

As individuals and teachers, we possess different strengths. Though we share common teaching philosophies and methods, we excel as individual teachers in different areas. Some may place emphasis on experiential learning activities while others may gravitate toward a more traditional lecture and discussion format. One teacher may enjoy integrating the latest technology while another may prefer community-based educational methods or integrating the arts in teaching. Individuals who identify with the left brain, or analytical ways of thinking and being in the world, will necessarily approach teaching differently than those who identify with the right brain, or creative processes. Good or effective teaching, after all, takes on many forms. And though we should certainly strive to develop and hone all aspects of our craft, we can nonetheless recognize and honor our respective strengths.

Likewise, your specific personal and educational background can be leveraged in the preparation of your WLSP course. A teacher with a background in applied linguistics has a different and equally valid perspective on and approach to WLSP as one with a degree in cultural studies or literature. A linguist, for example, might choose to foreground theoretical issues in the teaching of translation and interpreting, placing emphasis on the sorts of ethical decisions interpreters might face in practice. A teacher with a background in cultural studies specializing in the Latinx population in the United States, for example, might instead choose to foreground the role of culture in interpreting and the ways in which culture informs interpreter choices and the quality and experience of service (medical, legal, etc.) for the Latinx population. Furthermore, many individuals have multiple degrees, certificates, or specializations in different areas, such as international business, nursing, translation and interpreting, music, dance, art, film, and education, among others. A Japanese teacher with a background in cultural studies and gender and with administrative experience in higher education might build a lesson or class around their professional interests in administration, focusing on gender norms, inequalities, or other issues. Likewise, a German teacher with a background in literature and with professional experience in diplomatic interpreting might also design a lesson or course that contextualizes and historically situates cultural issues in diplomatic interpreting through literary texts.

In the same way, personal backgrounds significantly inform perspective and approach in lesson planning and curriculum development. An individual of Spanish origin, for example, may have a different cultural orientation and focus than one from Latin America, a heritage learner, or nonnative Spanish speaker. One Spaniard may want to address health care from a global and transnational perspective, for example, focusing on the role of migrants in hospice care and childcare, while an Argentine may want to focus on differences in the health care provider system, and a US-born Latinx may want to examine local issues and cultural differences in Latinx experiences with health services in the United States. Furthermore, the multiplicity of identities and social and cultural experiences evident across the Spanish speaking world and within the broad umbrellas designated by the terms "heritage language learner" and "nonnative Spanish speaker" make for a rich tapestry of perspectives that can be drawn upon to inform curricular choices in WLSP. Differences in nationality, region, language and culture, social identities, socioeconomic background, age, religion, ethnicity, race, and other sociocultural factors come into play when designing and giving a lesson or course, whether we are aware of it or not. This means that each and every individual has a unique story and perspective that can be resourced to enrich the teaching and learning experience.

Beyond our training and personal and professional backgrounds, many of us have unique interests, passions, motivations, and areas expertise that may have little or nothing to do with our professional lives. How might these inform curricular choices? Do you have a passion for documentary film? Are you a blogger, vlogger (video logger), or podcaster? Do you have a personal business on the side? Are you a ballroom, swing, Latin, or hip-hop dancer? Do you enjoy cooking or baking? Do you host a radio program or have experience with radio, television, or film? Believe it or not, all of these hobbies, interests, pastimes, or extracurriculars can be resourced and brought into the classroom. When it comes to integrating such extracurricular personal passions and interests, the possibilities are limited only by your imagination.

Recognizing your personal and professional strengths and interests will serve as a base from which to begin building lesson plans and curricula in WLSP. Most importantly, doing so will also allow you to proceed with confidence. These attributes influence how we teach in that they inform the choices we make in curriculum development and in course delivery and assessment. Though perhaps impossible to quantify, it makes sense that being aware of this fact and making conscious curricular decisions based on this knowledge can only enhance learning outcomes and the learning experience. At the very least, it allows for a more thoughtful, integrated, and cohesive lesson and class that also enables significant learning and the advancement of world language learning objectives.

Perhaps the most important reason to leverage your background, training, and professional experience/interests is the ability to advance broader language learning objectives related to intercultural competence. It is important to recognize that what allows you to link your background and training with WLSP content and objectives is culture. Indeed, it is *the* link that makes possible the transdisciplinarity of the field itself. Beyond the development of preprofessional knowledge, skills, and vocabulary, an emphasis on culture—beginning with the cultural perspective you as the teacher bring to the lesson and class—allows students to make personally meaningful connections across cultures and with relevant social issues. Furthermore, it is through this bridging of culture that students will develop intercultural competence and the broader transcultural and translingual objectives espoused by the MLA and ACTFL. Why is this important? Regardless of whether our students use their language skills and knowledge in a professional capacity after graduation, they will be better equipped to serve, lead, and otherwise contribute to making their local communities and the world a better, more compassionate place.

Leveraging Classroom, Campus, and Community Resources
Classroom

There is an abundance of resources at your disposal within the classroom, campus, and greater community. Your students are perhaps your greatest and most immediate assets. Assuming that the course or lesson in question includes intermediate to advanced students, the classroom will likely consist of majors, minors, and other qualifying students interested in the topic. They too will evidence a diversity of personal and educational backgrounds, professional experience, interests, and passions. Though difficult to plan for initially, knowing your students, or at least the general type of students within your department and institution, and what they might potentially contribute to the classroom dynamic will go a long way toward creating lessons that will be engaging, effective, and personally relevant.

Adapting courses and lessons to the students requires creativity and forethought. The objectives and content of the lesson need not necessarily change, but the focus, classroom activities, service-learning opportunities, and assessments might. To begin, reflect on the following questions:

- What type of students does our program or this class attract? Are they undergraduates, graduates, majors, minors, or students from other departments?
- What is the typical or current demographic makeup of the program or class? Are there heritage learners?
- What is the typical professional track for our students? Are they preparing for graduate work in world languages, careers in academia, business, medicine, education, or other?
- What educational backgrounds do they typically possess? Are they international business, premed, education, or nursing students?
- What prior professional or preprofessional experience might they have?
- What unique interests, hobbies, skills, and passions might they bring?

Teaching a course on translation and interpreting for commerce to advanced undergraduates and graduates as a part of a certificate program in international business at a middle tier research institution poses different opportunities than a lesson on the same topic for undergraduate majors in a course on linguistics at a small liberal arts college. It would be reasonable to assume that students in the former example would bring a greater diversity of educational and personal backgrounds in addition to actual professional experience in their respective career interests. There may even be a wide range of age differences and life experiences. In the latter case, it would likewise be a safe assumption that the students would be a more homogenous group consisting of majors and minors with little or no professional experience and preparing for careers in education or for further graduate work in world languages, possibly linguistics, and other related fields, such as anthropology, medicine, education, or international relations. In both instances, you might expect to see a mix of heritage and second-language (L2) learners.

Once you identify the type of students in your class, consider how they might contribute to the classroom and how you might adapt the course or lesson to speak to their respective strengths. In both instances, adjustments in teaching methodology will serve to make the most of your students' strengths. For example, whatever the respective backgrounds, education, professional experience, and interests of your students, build space into your syllabus, assignments, activities, or assessments for them to build on and share their knowledge and experience. Reflection journal assignments and essay questions, personalized projects, service learning, class presentations, and group work all provide opportunities for students to make connections between what they are learning and what they already know. Exactly how to integrate these is discussed in later chapters. For the purposes of this chapter, suffice it to say that there are innumerable ways to allow for students to contribute to the class and to their learning without modifying the content of the course.

In the case that you would like the course or lesson to speak directly to your students' strengths, however, content changes may also be necessary. Teaching a course on medical Spanish for nonmajors in a nursing program made up of mostly heritage learners and advanced L2 students, for example, may present an opportunity to include content relevant to the nursing profession and that addresses Latinx culture and the specific health care needs of the Latinx population in the United States. This might differ from a more general course on the same topic but offered for majors and minors in Spanish hoping to enter graduate school or teach Spanish at the secondary level. Granted, there will be overlap in content across these two scenarios, but the former allows for greater depth of study and discussion specific to the needs and challenges of nursing students. Here too, experiential and reflective teaching methods will serve to maximize student learning.

Campus

The campus community is another potential resource for developing WLSP curricula. Depending on the type of institution, there may be colleagues within the language department or in other departments with expertise or interest in collaborating, research centers and degree or certificate programs of relevance, and outreach programs or coordinators (e.g., a study abroad office or community-based education support staff). Understandably so, it is not unusual for faculty to become so engrossed in the immediate demands of their job and department that they know little about their neighbors, opportunities, and support across campus. Identifying and engaging them requires time and effort, but the benefits to your course or lesson planning are well worth it.

Among others, consider the following questions to begin brainstorming possible on-campus resources:

- What resources exist within my department?
- What other degree programs or certificate programs on campus might be of relevance?
- Are there any faculty members within my department or across campus with relevant expertise or interest who might be willing to collaborate?
- What research and learning centers and other teaching and outreach support services might be beneficial in course development?
- What opportunities exist within my department and across campus for the development of new courses or certificates in WLSP?

From there, the possibilities depend on the resources available and the willingness to collaborate and bring them to fruition. Does the college have a vibrant radio station or radio, television, and film program that could be resourced in developing courses and lessons in WLSP? Are there faculty in the business, medicine, or law programs who might be interested in collaborating, giving guest presentations, or at least sharing information, community and professional contacts, and resources? What opportunities are there to develop WLSP courses for study abroad? Might there be an opportunity to develop undergraduate or graduate certificates in WLSP in collaboration with other programs and departments on campus? How you approach these conversations will depend on the dynamics, culture, and politics of your department and campus, but doing so is a crucial step in developing WLSP curricula.

Community

Lastly, the local community provides a rich resource for WLSP that is only recently being explored by world language scholars, specifically in the way of community partnerships, service-learning, and internships. Whether a vibrant metropolitan area or a small rural town, every community offers a unique wealth of resources for teachers and students in WLSP. As with the campus resources, however, it will take time and effort to identify them, develop partnerships, and assess how best to integrate them into the course and curriculum. Doing so is likewise well worth the effort as it allows for students to make real-world connections with what they are learning in WLSP.

As with the other sections, consider the following questions as a general point of departure:

- What are the demographics of the local community and surrounding area?
- What are the professional and service needs of the city and target language population?
- What businesses, local organizations, centers, and institutions serve the target language population?

- What industries, organizations, or institutions are prominently associated with the city?
- What partnerships currently exist between the campus and community?

The city of Memphis, Tennessee, for example, is known as a diverse city with a growing immigrant and immigrant descendant population from Latin America, Asia, and Africa, among other areas. Industry wise, the city is associated with major corporations like FedEx and Autozone, tourism, and medicine with the Saint Jude's Children's Hospital. As to be expected, various organizations, centers, and businesses reflect the needs and culture of the city's population. With regard to the Latinx community, these include the *Centro Cultural Latino de Memphis*, Latino Memphis, and *La Prensa Latina*, among others. For a Spanish teacher wishing to develop community partnerships in WLSP, there would be ample opportunity to do so in a city such as Memphis.

Similarly, the small rural town of Monmouth, Illinois, is equally demographically diverse. Associated with the college by the same name and a meat packing plant, the town is home to agriculturalists, meat packing factory workers, students from the Midwest, and faculty members from across the nation. Interestingly, the meat packing plant attracts workers from Latin America and Francophone Africa, making for a unique culture and language mixture of Spanish, indigenous languages from Mexico, and French. By 2012, the distinctive needs of this diverse population were only beginning to be assessed and met by the college and local governmental services. A world language teacher in such an environment would similarly have ample opportunity to develop and integrate community partnerships.

Even in those instances where a population in the target language is not readily accessible, study abroad and technology present opportunities for community engagement. Strategies for doing so are discussed in a later chapter. For the purposes of this chapter, suffice it to say that the resources that do exist in the community can still be leveraged to your advantage. Beyond service learning, teachers may consider, for example, supplementing or complementing courses and lessons in WLSP with broader discussions and explorations of immigration and language and culture issues in the local community. What perspective might a health service provider focused on the medical needs of one immigrant population bring to a broader and comparative discussion on the topic of language, culture, and health? Inviting such a speaker or developing a lesson plan using the service provider and community in question as a case study might provide a valuable learning experience for the students. Granted, doing so requires additional work on the part of the teacher and students in bridging the topic, but it may enrich student understanding of the concepts and advance learning objectives. In addition, it allows for students to make real-world connections.

4

Curriculum Development
for the WLSP Classroom

THIS CHAPTER PROVIDES AN overview of general issues in curriculum development for the WLSP classroom and lesson plan. With the exception of the topic
and objectives, the teaching of WLSP is no different than that of any other subject
within world languages. Indeed, there are many excellent resources in world language higher education pedagogy, and this chapter, as well as the others in this book,
are intended to be used in tandem with existing pedagogical materials and courses.
That said, and given the specialized nature of WLSP, there is an opportunity here to
rethink the why and how of world language teaching at the higher education level.

As noted in the previous chapters, the goal of WLSP and world language higher
education in general is to better prepare students for the global world into which they
are entering upon graduation. WLSP teachers will have the benefit of helping them
build specific language, professional, and life skills founded on goals and objectives
that transcend the classroom. Based on my experience in developing, researching,
and teaching WLSP topics and courses, this chapter is designed to help you orient your curriculum development in WLSP toward these objectives. Indeed, having
familiarized yourself with the resources at your disposal in the ways suggested in the
previous chapter, you might naturally ask how to begin building learning objectives,
course materials, syllabi and calendars, lesson plans, assignments, and assessments
for the WLSP classroom. How to integrate WLSP topics into existing composition,
conversation, literature, culture, and basic language sequence courses in the standard
world language curriculum are addressed in chapter 7.

Learning Objectives

Developing learning objectives for WLSP courses and lessons is no different than
developing them for other language courses, be they literature, cultural studies, or
linguistics. Regardless of the course and topic, for example, they should align with
current standards in world language education as identified by such organizations
as the ACTFL and the MLA. That said, teachers and students should bear in mind
that teaching and learning objectives in WLSP encompass and seek to integrate two

related areas, now also advocated as central to language learning in general: language development and intercultural competence. In the first instance, specialized vocabulary and grammar along with preprofessional training are the primary focus, while awareness and application of cultural knowledge, cultural heterogeneity, and intercultural sensitivity in specialized contexts are those of the second. Just as with the communicative approach to language learning, it is understood that specialized language skills can be acquired alongside intercultural competence through situated and immersive learning opportunities, such as professional internships, CSL, and other community-based education initiatives. Thus, lesson plans and courses in WLSP typically contain both aspects of these learning objectives.

Considering the two related learning objective areas of WLSP, the language used in writing them should include content as well as concept- and process-centered words and expressions. For example, a course on languages for commerce might include the following objectives, following the ACTFL's "Can-Do-Statements":

By the end of the course, students can

- Identify commerce-specific vocabulary and grammar.
- Acquire preprofessional training.
- Recognize diverse cultural approaches to commerce and communication within professional business contexts.
- Compare and contrast diverse cultural approaches to commerce and communication within professional business contexts.
- Demonstrate effective and appropriate use of commerce-specific vocabulary and grammar, cultural knowledge, and preprofessional skills in a cross-cultural communicative business context.

The five objectives listed here encompass the major learning goals of WLSP while allowing for the integration and development of the 5 C's of the ACTFL's World Readiness Standards (communication, cultures, connections, comparisons, communities). These same objectives can also be adapted and applied to almost any course and even lesson plan in WLSP. In sum, consider what specialized language skills you are teaching, what specialized skills you are providing, and how you intend to foster cultural awareness and intercultural competence. These will be your guiding framework for writing WLSP course and lesson objectives.

Teaching and Learning Resources and Materials

There are two main points that should be addressed with regard to teaching materials in WLSP: the first is what to do about existing learning materials, and the second has to do with new ideas coming from other areas outside of languages. There are many materials and other resources available for teachers and students to use in developing their new courses. The final chapter of this book contains a list of some of these resources. For the purposes of this chapter, suffice it to say that many of the existing materials and resources are helpful as a starting point for developing your own teaching materials. Just as with any other subject, teachers need not reinvent the wheel, so to speak, but they will need to be creative as to how they will use or integrate these materials and resources into their existing and new courses.

Learning objectives for the course or lesson will ultimately inform your choice of materials and resources as well as how you use them. A book such as this one, for example, can be used to provide the framework for a course on WLSP pedagogy and can be supplemented with additional articles, books, or book chapters, or it can serve as a supplement in a general world language pedagogy course. Likewise, the models and examples provided in this book or other similar WLSP books might be adapted for use in specific lesson plans focusing on WLSP and related topics. How you choose to incorporate the texts and other materials is a matter of choice but should always be in alignment with the objectives of the course and lesson.

The second point concerns how teachers think about and integrate those materials. How we choose to adopt other resources outside of the language curriculum is important to consider because it can make a tremendous impact on how students understand and integrate the material in their own language development and in the development of their person beyond academics and language skills.

There is much outside of the language curriculum that could be integrated. There are many philosophies and traditions of thinking that challenge the current status quo, for example, and that could be used to supplement teacher and student understanding of the materials and of the current situation in which they find themselves in terms of history, culture, politics, economics, and so forth. This is fundamental to breaking free from the current paradigm that we have established in our education system in general, and it is necessary in order to transform the world language curriculum in this new century we are in. In short, feel free to integrate sources and perspectives from other areas as you see fit. As a general rule, however, course and lesson plan objectives will determine both the what and how of material and resource selection and integration. In summary, consider the following questions when assessing possible materials and resources:

- What is it that I need in order to teach this particular lesson or approach this teaching and learning objective?
- What resources are in existence, print, online, and community?
- What additional and potentially relevant print, online, and community resources outside of WLSP may be relevant and useful to the teaching of this course or lesson learning objectives?
- How might I best leverage existing resources to support my course and lesson learning objectives?

We are on the verge of redefining world language education, and it is to our benefit to integrate as many new and fundamentally transformational ideas as possible, as unpopular as this idea may seem to staunch academics and to mainstream politicians in our world today.

Syllabi and Calendars
Developing course syllabi and calendars is also no different than developing them for other courses in WLSP, but they do differ in terms of how teachers choose to structure and integrate WLSP. There are two ways in which we can approach this in WLSP. We can either choose to integrate WLSP lessons into existing courses

or we can develop new courses in WLSP. In the first case, we need to think about whether our program needs are being met by the existing courses and whether we need to update them by integrating WLSP or such community-based initiatives as CSL. This can be done within WLSP and also within non-WLSP courses. It just depends on what the needs and available resources are within the program and within the community. You should choose existing courses that fit well with the goals and objectives of WLSP, including making students better people through language and culture courses and instruction.

There are several questions you want to consider when creating new WLSP courses and curriculum materials. First and foremost, you need to think about the needs of the students as well as about the needs of the program. What are the students interested in? What are they studying, what are their backgrounds, what languages do they speak, where did they grow up, what career interests do they have, etc., etc.? These are not trivial questions to entertain; they are fundamental to building a course and program that reflects and speaks to the needs of the students and the communities from which they come. This is one of the main goals and objectives of WLSP: to meet the needs of students and communities through purposeful instruction in languages and cultures within specific contexts.

Now there are other factors that ought to be considered as well. The first thing you may want to consider is whether there are existing courses that can contribute in some way to the goals and objectives of WLSP. A literature or culture course may be well suited to integrating WLSP topics, objectives, aims, and so forth. If this is the case, there may be no need to develop specific courses in WLSP. If, on the other hand, there are no such courses that can support WLSP objectives, you will need to create new courses specifically in WLSP. You will need to then think of what the needs are of the students and the community. For example, do students at University X or Y want to study medicine, law enforcement, or education, or what are their primary educational and career interests? What opportunities exist within the community to support their interests, or, by extension, how might the university resources and student interests speak to the needs of the community? These can be leveraged in the creation of new courses and will go a long way toward ensuring their success, relevance, and value for students, the program, and the community.

Lesson Plans

There are two things you need to keep in mind when designing lesson plans in WLSP. The first is that you need to be mindful of the resources you have available to you in the department and also in the community. The second is that you need to pay attention to the needs of your students. When your students tell you they want to learn about language for medicine, law enforcement, or for entrepreneurial activities, listen to them and find a way to integrate it into your lesson plan. When students communicate with their teachers about their learning needs, they often do so out of a need for recognition. Whether they actually know what they need is a whole other question, but you can at least entreat their interests and requests and consider whether they will work within the course and lesson plan you have designed.

Lesson plans should be free of jargon. This is to say that while theory should inform your approach to WLSP, it should not be the primary focus in teaching. In addition, there should be no grammar or vocabulary or anything of that sort that does not support the objectives of the lesson. In other words, what you are teaching is not theory, grammar, or even vocabulary but a specific way of using the language that involves words and grammatical structures, yes, but goes far beyond that to encompass body language, other nonverbal forms of communication, and culture in so far as culture informs communication and interpretation of meaning.

With the exception of the topic, a lesson plan in WLSP will differ little from those of other language and culture courses. A well-designed lesson plan, for example, will include all the same elements one might expect in any language course, including clear objectives and innovative learning methods and techniques incorporating a mixture of instruction or lecture/presentation and comprehension and language reproduction activities situated within specific cultural and professional or other sociocultural contexts. A lesson may also include and even revolve around cultural texts, such as literature, audio-visual materials, cultural expressions (e.g., music, dance, art), and material culture, may integrate technology, and may incorporate experiential learning activities such as games, role-play, conversation, writing activities, group work, presentations, and so forth. Regardless of the specific activities chosen, an ideal lesson plan will foreground and integrate culture throughout. This means that an ideal lesson plan will move from an approximation of the topic from the broader lens of culture to the teaching of specific language learning objectives (i.e., vocabulary and grammar) in context and back again to a reflection on how language, culture, and the topic in question intersect.

Two sample lesson plans for WLSP-specific courses following this schema are included in the appendix. Though they are specifically designed for Spanish for commerce and Spanish for health care, they are intended to serve as models and as a practical guide for developing lesson plan ideas across any language and topic. They are also flexible in terms of time scale, meaning the lesson plans can serve for a single class period, an entire week, or a whole unit. In addition, specific accompanying readings or assigned texts are likewise omitted. These ambiguities are intentional and are intended to accommodate the varying range of time and resources available to world language teachers across the higher education landscape. That said, a list of selected textbook recommendations for different language areas and WLSP topics are provided in the appendix.

Given the specific topic in question, WLSP lessons may also include such community-based learning activities as CSL or in-class or on-site presentations by community partners. In such cases, the lesson plan will take into consideration the objectives of the service learning projects and community partners. How to do this is addressed in chapters 5 and 6. For now, suffice it to say that lesson planning in WLSP needs to be flexible and responsive to the needs of the course, students, and any community partners. Indeed, a given course and lesson can be approached, designed, and taught any number of ways depending on the creativity, resources, and aims and objectives of the teacher. As noted in chapter 3, resources for profession-specific vocabulary abound, and a lack of education, training, or work experience in the specific topic of the course or lesson in question need not deter teachers of any background from undertaking development of courses and lesson plans in WLSP.

Regardless of the final form of the lesson plan, the primary objective must be the development of student intercultural sensitivity and cultural and communicative competence. As noted, this is done by situating language learning within a broader cultural lens and framework and by including reflection as an integral part of learning. The lesson plans provided in the appendix and the assignments discussed next provide a few examples of how teachers can facilitate student reflection. For the purposes of this section, however, know that any given lesson plan should integrate some form of student reflection, if only through discussion. This will allow students the opportunity to synthesize and integrate the new information learned in class with their existing knowledge and experience. The significance of this cannot be stressed enough and is crucial to achieving the broader goals and objectives of WLSP and of a new and transformed language curriculum for this next century.

Assignments

Likewise, assignments should be reflective of the goals and objectives of the lesson plans and of WLSP in general. You should keep the focus on the objectives outlined in the lesson plan and should keep the focus on learning from a heart-centered perspective, as outlined in the first part of this book. There are two things to take into consideration here. The first is that you need to pay attention to what the needs of your students are. The second is that you need to be mindful of what your department and community needs are.

As with lesson planning, the types of assignments can vary considerably in a WLSP course and reflect best practices in language teaching in general. As such, this section addresses two specific types of assignments that work especially well in a WLSP context: reflection journals and pragmatic assignments. In both instances, the teacher needs to be mindful of the objectives outlined in the lesson plan and should keep the focus on learning from a heart-centered perspective, as outlined in the first part of this book. This is to say that language-learning objectives (i.e., vocabulary and grammar) should be reinforced through practical exercises that also allow for reflection and the integration of new and previous knowledge.

Three assignments are provided in the appendix as examples and guides: a reflection journal (Spanish for law enforcement), an interpreter exercise (medical Spanish context), and a composition exercise (Spanish for commerce context). The reflection journal can be used in any course, regardless of topic, and is useful in allowing students to make personal connections with the course topic, materials, assignments, and discussions. It is also helpful in bridging the culture and community gap in courses that are otherwise focused on language development (i.e., vocabulary acquisition). You are welcome to exercise creativity and flexibility in constructing your journal assignments and prompts. How you grade such an assignment, however, depends on your objectives. Placing emphasis on composition may be effective at the intermediate and advance levels, but may interfere with the broader purpose of the journal. A completion grade with corrections to student composition may be a better option for less advanced and other courses. Likewise, the journals could be redesigned as a digital vlog (video log) for conversation courses. Regardless of the form of the journal, reflection must be at the center of the assignment. Types of assessments, including for assignments, will be considered further next.

The interpreter and composition assignments likewise allow for critical reflection, though in a more focused way that reinforces specific language learning objectives. The interpreter assignment can be tailored for use with any of the medical language units or modules. This assignment forces students to move beyond reproduction of content to the practical application of learned language skills. Students will therefore reinforce what they have learned in class in accomplishing a task, albeit controlled and modified, that might be expected of them in a professional context. The composition exercise likewise achieves this in applying the students' acquired knowledge of business and profession-specific vocabulary and grammar toward the composition of a job application cover letter. Ideally, such an assignment should be tailored to the students' actual professional career goals. Of significance, both the interpreter and the composition exercises also allow students to build on what they have learned in class by integrating previous knowledge, personal interests, and real-world problem-solving tasks (how to appropriately interpret speech and how to communicate your professional and personal experience in an appropriate and professional way).

It should be noted that textbooks, when available, often provide exercises and assignments, many of which can be done online. This trend is likely to increase in the near future as more WLSP materials are created and technology and education continue to merge. You are encouraged to take advantage of these innovations. You are also encouraged, however, to use your creativity and ingenuity in designing your own assignments or modifying existing ones found in textbooks (including this one) or other sources as a means of better suiting the assignments to the needs of your students, program, and learning objectives. This is to say that assignments, as all course materials from the objectives and syllabi to assessments, ought to reflect the specific needs and strengths of the teacher, students, program, institution, and community.

Assessments

There are two things you need to know in order to write assessments in WLSP. The first thing you need to know is that there are two basic types of assessments in WLSP. The first is a test or exam type of assessment that assesses student mastery of topics. The second is a type of exam that assesses student-learning abilities such as learning how to learn and learning how to learn a language (see King de Ramirez and Lafford 2013). You want to use the second type of assessment as much as possible in order to achieve what is called significant learning (see Fink 2003; Ruggiero 2019). This type of learning is that which goes beyond the learning of topics and objectives, such as language vocabulary and language grammar skills, and encompasses metacognition, attitudes, and intercultural sensitivity and competence, among other affective domains involved in the learning process.

It should be noted that the learning process is a way of learning that goes beyond anything that can be objectively assessed by current assessment measures, such as tests, quizzes, or exams. This is because no one has yet to devise a way of assessing mastery of the learning process itself. Furthermore, standard assessment tools such as surveys, tests, quizzes, exams, and journals are imperfect even in assessing student learning outcomes because they only show what a person is thinking at the moment and not what they have actually learned or the learning process itself. There is a way, however, to assess how students perform at a given assignment or task like a challenge. Such tasks often referred to as problem- or project-based learning activities, are a central component of significant learning and are increasingly being used in education in general. In all cases, the use of rubrics are the best means of assessing and providing students with the feedback they need in order to evaluate their own growth and progress.

An example of a significant learning assessment in the form of a midterm or final exam is provided in the appendix. The basic structure of the exam can be modified for shorter unit tests. The exam consists of four general types of questions grouped into three or four separate sections, moving from facts and concepts to comparative questions and real-world problem-solving scenarios and reflexive essays. This format allows students to demonstrate what they have learned in multiple ways. Mastery of foundational knowledge, which will often consist of short answer and comparative questions, is necessary for language learning at any level of language proficiency. Yet, incorporating problem solving and reflexive essays allows students to show their mastery of those same foundational skills in synthesizing and integrating that information with their prior knowledge and personal background and educational and professional experience. Much like the journals, the reflexive essay questions, if used, provide teachers a means of better understanding how students are understanding and thinking about the topic or issues in question and how they are integrating that information on a personal or affective level.

5

Developing Community Partnerships for CSL in WLSP

THIS CHAPTER IS ABOUT identifying and fostering community partnerships for CSL in WLSP. A form of community-based education, CSL is increasingly used across the world language curriculum and is particularly suited to the aims and objectives of WLSP (Barreneche and Ramos-Flores 2013; Hellebrandt and Varona 1999; Lear 2012; Ruggiero 2015, 2018b; Sánchez-López 2013b). This is precisely because it allows students to bridge what they are learning in the classroom with the real world and apply their knowledge and skills in ways that advance their educational, professional, and personal growth (M. Long 2017b; Sánchez-López 2013b). In other words, it helps to contextualize and give meaning, purpose, and value to their education beyond a certificate or degree in a way that serves the community and informs their confidence, sense of self-worth, empathy, compassion, and way of engaging the world. These are bold words, but the literature on CSL increasingly underscores the broader value and benefits of CSL for student self-esteem and intercultural sensitivity and competence (e.g., Lafford, Abbott, and Lear 2014; King de Ramírez 2016, 2017; McBride 2010; Medina and Gordon 2014; Petrov 2013; Ruggiero 2016, 2017b, 2017c, 2018a, 2018b). If the broader goal of higher education in the twenty-first century is to create future leaders who are curious, empathic, compassionate, conscientious, and interculturally competent, then it stands to reason that taking learning outside of the classroom and engaging the community through CSL and other community-based education initiatives is an absolute imperative. Furthermore, the value of CSL for providing much needed outreach and assistance to immigrant and underserved communities is underscored by the 2020 COVID-19 pandemic. The extreme challenges presented by social distancing to designing and implementing CSL in WLSP are unique and are thus addressed in a separate chapter. Even before designing a WLSP-specific CSL project, whether face-to-face or virtual, teachers will need to foster and develop community partnerships (Abbott and Lear 2010; Lear 2012; Lear and Abbott 2009; Lear and Sánchez 2013; Ruggiero 2018c).

Next, you will find practical strategies for identifying and fostering community partners for CSL projects in WLSP based on my experience developing CSL projects for WLSP as well as on current best practices in WLSP-based CSL. This information is particularly helpful for those with no prior experience in CSL, though it also serves others currently using CSL in expanding and reinforcing existing projects.

Identifying and Fostering Community Partnerships and CSL Projects

Perhaps the most daunting part of undertaking a CSL project is simply getting started. Where to find resources, especially in the community, is often a concern (Abbott and Lear 2010; Lear and Abbott 2009; Ruggiero and Hill 2016). This is especially the case for those who find themselves teaching in locations where there may be a small or seemingly invisible community of the target language and where there are few or no apparent businesses, organizations, or other institutions serving the needs of that population (Abbott and Lear 2010). Finding viable community partnerships and CSL projects in such cases can prove challenging, but there are ways around these issues, some of which are alluded to in chapter 3 and are considered further in this chapter. Regardless of the resources available, this section addresses ways in which teachers can begin to identify and foster community partnerships and potential CSL projects.

Even before thinking about what sorts of projects students might be able to undertake as a part of CSL, teachers must first identify and foster community partnerships. Why? Because CSL implies a partnership between you as a representative of your institution and a community-based business, organization, institution, service provider, or other such entity. This means that you and the community partner will ideally enter into a service-learning agreement that is mutually beneficial to all parties (Lear and Abbott 2009). By extension, this means that good and sustainable community partnerships are ones that are built on collaboration and that are essentially equitable (Ruggiero 2018c). This is, in part, what distinguishes service learning from other forms of community-based education, such as internships. In an equitable and collaborative CSL project, the learning needs and objectives of the student are met, as are the needs and objectives of the community partners. As a result, the needs of the community and objectives of the educational institution are also served. In short, it is a mutually beneficial partnership that meets multiple needs. This is what helps to make service learning such a meaningful experience for students, teachers, community partners, and institutions of higher learning.

Meeting such lofty goals may seem daunting at first, but what you need to consider first and foremost are the learning objectives for the course and work your way out to the community (Lear and Abbott 2009; King de Ramírez 2017; Ruggiero 2018c). For example, if teaching a course on language for commerce, you want to consider the overall objectives and goals of the course. Included among them may be providing students with profession-specific vocabulary and language skills as well as preprofessional training and experience and fostering intercultural competence. From there, consider what resources exist at your institution and in the community that might support your learning objectives. Is there an office, committee, person, or webpage designated for community engagement and outreach at your campus? If not, are there online resources to help you get started and generate ideas, whether through organizations like the ACTFL or institutions that champion community engagement? Perhaps there is a fellow colleague in your department or in another department who has experience with community outreach or community engagement and who might be willing to help or collaborate? If such resources exist, they will likely provide support, models, and contacts of existing or potential community partners. For this reason, and so as not to reinvent the wheel, this needs to be your first point of departure. If no such resources exist, then you will necessarily need to go out into the community directly to see what opportunities for partnerships and projects exist.

Much of community outreach and engagement begins at an interpersonal level (Lear and Abbott 2009; Ruggiero 2018c). This means that, unless you have existing partnerships previously established through your institution, you will need to go out into the community and establish relationships. Only by being present and involved in, or at least engaged with, your local community can you get a sense for what partnership and project opportunities exist. If you are in an area with a visible target language community, seek out businesses, organizations, and service providers serving the needs of that population. Consider the following questions:

- Is the target language population concentrated in certain neighborhoods or areas of the community?
- Are there local businesses owned and operated by individuals of the target language?
- Are there cultural organizations representing the cultural heritage and diversity of the target language?
- Are there organizations and institutions that serve the educational, health care, legal, immigrant, labor, childcare, religious/spiritual, and other needs of the target language population?
- What about larger institutions such as hospitals and other organizations such as nonprofits that service a larger community but that still need assistance in providing bilingual services or outreach to the target language population?

Also consider businesses in the area whose labor pool is predominantly of the target language population. What opportunities might there be to partner with them? Only by asking such questions, being present in the community, and forming interpersonal relationships can you begin to make sense of the local cultural landscape and therefore of the opportunities that exist for CSL and other community-based outreach initiatives.

Being present in the community can take many forms, but getting to know people is the most important thing you can do. Volunteering your time and energy and joining directorship boards is one way to achieve this end, but it can and should go beyond this. Visit local businesses, organizations, and institutions, go to local events, and get to know your neighbors. Talk to people, and not just those who own and operate or work there, but also the people who frequent and use the services of those places. What are their individual stories or organizational missions? What challenges do they face as business or service providers attempting to meet the needs of the local population? What challenges do community members face in having their personal, health care, childcare, labor, educational, legal, and other needs met in this city, county, and country? What needs are being met successfully, unsuccessfully, or not at all? In short, get to know them.

As you begin to develop a sense of what the local demographics are and of the opportunities for partnerships, you can begin to form ideas about potential partnerships that could provide CSL projects best suited to the learning objectives of your course. A partnership with a local business or institution owned by, or at least catering to, the needs of the target language population is ideal for a language for commerce course, for instance. Likewise, a community organization focused on providing affordable health care to local immigrants or a large hospital seeking to engage in outreach and education to the non-English speaking population are good partners for a language for health care course. Local law enforcement agencies and community organizations likewise engaged in outreach and education efforts or in need of translating and interpreting services are viable partners as well.

In the event that a shortage of a population in the target language or of businesses and service providers exists in your area, CSL partnerships and projects are still possible (Ruggiero and Hill 2016). One possibility is to travel to the nearest metropolitan or other area where a denser population exists. Yet another idea is broadening the scope of the CSL project beyond language acquisition and the target language population to address issues in language, culture, and community more generally. In other words, a course on language for health care may integrate a CSL project in which students engage with a community health organization or institution servicing the needs of the local immigrant population (any language). Even though the students might not necessarily be using their target language skills in the project itself, they would still gain invaluable insight into the real world challenges facing health care providers and local immigrants. This could serve as a valuable complement to what the students are learning in the course and could still help bridge the classroom-community divide. Such an experience also furthers the objective of developing intercultural sensitivity and competence. Lastly, if on a campus with a significant number of heritage learners of the target language, consider designing a service-learning project that meets the needs of the campus community. In such an instance, it may still be possible to partner with a community organization to address a specific business, health, or wellness need on campus. Though a twist on the traditional idea of CSL where students go out of the institution, it is important to remember that community also includes the campus.

Yet another solution involves technology. CSL often connotes face-to-face engagement and contact with local communities. The reality, however, is that, with the help of radio and online tools and platforms such as Google Drive, YouTube, Skype, and social media, you can partner with an organization in another place, including another region, state, or country, to create service-learning opportunities that are equally as beneficial and meaningful for students, partners, and the communities served (e.g., King de Ramírez 2016; Ruggiero and Hill 2016). Students might engage directly or indirectly with the community and partners in question, in real-time or asynchronously. Just as with face-to-face service-learning scenarios, such projects could be an extension of existing organization outreach efforts or new and original collaborative projects. The project could involve governmental organizations, multinational corporations, international organizations, local organizations and businesses, or churches. Perhaps the easiest form of an online, and even face-to-face, project may be a webpage translation. Regardless of the partner or type of project, technology has allowed for an extension and reenvisioning of the concept of community, making possible virtual service learning. This point, as well as further strategies for developing virtual CSL projects in WLSP, is considered in greater detail in chapter 11.

In addition to these scenarios, service learning can also take place in a study abroad context. Many institutions that champion community engagement now include such service learning opportunities in countries around the world. Given the centrality of study abroad in world language education, there is an opportunity to expand our current language learning objectives to encompass WLSP and CSL objectives and fulfill institutional missions in international contexts. Given the real-world needs and challenges of many countries, community service would be welcomed and valued at many host institutions, even if organized apart from the formal language study abroad experience. Even if the service-learning component takes on the form of volunteer work, the experience, in a study abroad context, would be invaluable to the development of student language skills and intercultural competence.

In short, service-learning is possible anywhere, and all it takes is a little effort in getting to know the people where you live and who the students may potentially serve. Resources abound and are currently expanding. Some of these sources are contained in the final chapter of this book. In addition, be sure to inquire at your home institution about community engagement resources, like a dedicated office, staff member, or webpage. Institutions of higher learning have made community engagement a priority for this century, and world language programs are uniquely positioned to contribute to this agenda through WLSP and CSL.

6

Designing and Integrating WLSP CSL Projects

THIS CHAPTER IS ABOUT the nuts and bolts of designing and integrating WLSP CSL projects. There are several ways a CSL project can be designed and integrated into a WLSP course. Doing so supports the objectives of WLSP, higher education world language departments, and institutions of higher learning. Specifically, CSL bridges classroom learning with practice and the community, provides students with preprofessional training along with specialized language skills, and helps to develop cultural awareness and intercultural sensitivity and competence, among other objectives (Abbott and Rejane 2018, 40; Ruggiero 2019, 3; see also Lafford 2013; Lear 2012). Ultimately, how you design and integrate your project will depend on the learning objectives of the course, community and student needs, and the resources at your disposal. To assist you in this process, what follows is a discussion of basic types of CSL projects for WLSP, CSL project design considerations, and CSL and classroom learning integration.

Though by no means comprehensive, the suggestions and examples offered in this chapter are based on my research and design experience in CSL for WLSP. As such, they are intended as a starting point for CSL project design. For your convenience, a selected list of print and online resources in the area of CSL in WLSP are included at the end of this book. Though the focus of this chapter is on traditional, face-to-face CSL, the strategies and models presented here may also be adapted for virtual projects, as is addressed in a later chapter.

Types of CSL Projects in WLSP

In general, projects will take one of two major forms. The first and perhaps easiest to design is a volunteer- or internship-type project wherein students step into roles and responsibilities already identified by the institution, organization, or business (e.g., King de Ramírez 2017). The second is a more collaborative project in which students themselves may be cocreators alongside community partners and teachers and design new projects collaboratively identified (e.g., King de Ramírez 2016; Ruggiero 2018c). Examples of each are considered throughout this chapter, as well as provided in the appendix. Suffice it to say that both types of projects have merit and are beneficial in fulfilling student learning and community partner objectives.

In both instances, learning objectives for the course will need to be considered in the overall design of the project. A language for health care course partnering with a local nonprofit delivering affordable health care services to the underserved might, for example, take as some of its objectives the following:

- Applying health care specific language skills in a real-world professional setting
- Providing preprofessional experience and training
- Fostering intercultural sensitivity and competence

The community partner may then consider what its objectives for the project design might be in relation to its overall mission and existing needs and ongoing projects. Educational outreach, interpreting, and translation services for the non-English speaking population, for example, are likely to be priorities for such organizations. In such cases, there may be preidentified needs and existing outreach projects or programs that the organizations may need help with, such as translating print and online educational materials or interpreting for patient intakes during free health clinic hours. In such cases, the project might consist of students entering into and fulfilling the roles and responsibilities identified by the organization. How you design the project around the needs of the organization, however, depends specifically on the learning objectives, discussed in greater detail later.

In my experience designing CSL projects, I find that though requiring more time, collaboration, and creativity, the second type of project may be more fulfilling for community partner, students, and teacher alike. In this scenario, teacher and community partner collaborate on the design of a new rather than existing project (e.g., King de Ramírez 2016; Ruggiero 2018c). A brainstorming session between yourself and the organization and even a formal needs assessment may be necessary in order to identify needs not currently considered or addressed by the organization and potential projects that could begin to meet those needs. In keeping with the earlier example of language for health care and community health organization partnership, such a project might consist of an educational outreach project designed and delivered by the students in conjunction with the community partner. With the help of the students and teacher, the organization might realize that it could better reach the target language population by offering educational sessions in the target language at local events, churches, or other such gatherings drawing members of that community. On behalf and with the support of the organization, students could design and create educational resources about a specific topic, like nutrition and diabetes, and organize workshops or informational sessions to give at specific community events or gatherings.

There are two structural advantages of the second type of project. The first benefit is the potential for equity among all vested partners and for the sustainability of the partnership and project (Ruggiero 2018c). The second is that it can potentially involve all enrolled students in a single project (e.g., Julseth 2004; King de Ramírez 2016; Ruggiero 2018c). Indeed, the overall design of the project could essentially be a framework that allows for flexibility in terms of project form and direction with continued student, community partner, and teacher input and feedback. This implies the potential for the continuity and growth of a community partnership and project beyond the life of the course itself (Ruggiero 2018c). Thinking in terms of sustainability is beneficial to the overall goals and objectives not only of community partners, but also of the course, teacher, department, and institution. Indeed, a project could be designed in such a way as to integrate the students as a part of the collaborative and creative design of the project. The advantage of this is that students become personally invested in the project, and this, in turn, may likewise have positive benefits for student learning outcomes and the overall success of the project as suggested by my research on CSL in WLSP (see also King de Ramírez 2016; McBride 2010; Petrov 2013).

In comparison, the benefit of the first type of project, the volunteer or internship model, is in accommodating the specific professional career interests of the students through placement with different community partners. While the language for health care scenario lends itself to a group project, a language for commerce course might benefit from professional internship-like projects wherein students undertake individual projects with partners in their area of interest. The feasibility of such a project may depend on the community resources available, however, and it should be noted that a group project is just as feasible for such a course. Regardless of form, how you design and integrate the CSL project in relation to the course and learning objectives will determine the overall efficacy of the project.

CSL Project Design for WLSP

Once a community partner is identified and needs are assessed, you can begin to design the project in earnest. The following addresses major questions and issues that may arise in the process of creating a CSL project, including how to integrate a project into the course calendar, how to balance the classroom and service-learning experience, and how to assess student-learning outcomes.

Determining how much time to allocate for student engagement with the project is perhaps the first issue you will need to consider. Rather than an independent assignment that students undertake on their own time outside of class time, consider integrating the project into the course. This means building time into the course calendar for students to work with the community partner(s). How this looks will depend on the nature of the service-learning project itself, the needs of the community partner, logistics, and the limitations imposed by your academic institution on the maximum number of hours allowed for student involvement in CSL, among others. For example, you might devote a single class period per week or a portion of the semester to the service-learning project, depending on the factors noted here. This works for both individual internship-like and large-group CSL projects and has the advantage of balancing traditional and experiential learning in a way that, if done correctly, should not compromise the integrity of the course in terms of content and learning objectives.

Achieving a balanced learning experience can also be accomplished by how you use class time in relation to the project. Regardless of the type of project, you might want to reorient or develop the course calendar, lesson plan, course readings and content, assignments, and discussions to speak to or reflect the topics, questions, issues, and challenges students are likely to encounter in the service-learning experience. Though this requires prior planning, it is perhaps the best way of ensuring that students bridge what they are learning in the classroom with what they are experiencing in the community. Yet another way to accomplish this is to invite guest speakers either from the partnering organization or from other areas who can speak to the broader issues that students are likely facing in their projects. Similarly, you can ask students to research and present on issues and questions of relevance to the project and invite the class to participate in discussion. At the very least, however, plan to build in space for discussion and reflection if not in, then outside of class. A sample lesson plan is provided in the appendix for your convenience.

Assignments, and specifically those that allow for reflection, provide an opportunity for students to make meaningful bridges in CSL. Reflection journals, essays, in-class presentations, and portfolios are most useful during a service-learning project. Considering the time students will be devoting to the project itself, such assignments are not time consuming and can be approached in creative ways. Furthermore, they provide a space in which students can make meaningful personal connections not only across the campus-community divide, but also in relation to their prior knowledge and personal, educational, and professional interests, experiences, and training (see McBride 2010; Petrov 2013; Ruggiero 2016, 2017c, 2018a). This, in my view and experience, is crucial in fully integrating the CSL project into the class and achieving the broader goals and agenda of WLSP apart from the content-specific goals of the course. Examples of service-learning journal assignments are provided in the appendix for your convenience.

Assessing Student Learning and Community Partnership Objectives

Though not all of the benefits of CSL for students, community partners, and the community are measurable using standard assessment instruments, there are certain outcomes that can be assessed, specifically, those related to course learning objectives, project objectives, and community partner objectives, which will be related to but may extend beyond the project objectives. There are many ways in which to do this, and the examples provided in the appendix and discussed here are just a few. Doing so is in keeping with best practices in CSL design and assessment (see Bringle, Clayton, and Hatcher 2013), and is important for the growth of CSL projects, the well-being and sustainability of community partnerships, and professional development purposes.

Student learning objectives can be assessed through traditional assessment tools, such as assignments, quizzes, exams, and grading rubrics. Here is where the formalistic aspects relating to language and language learning will be assessed (e.g., grammar, vocabulary, register), just as in a regular classroom setting. For example, if teaching a course on language for commerce in which learning objectives include acquisition of profession-specific vocabulary and appropriate and effective use of register in a professional context, assignments previously discussed, such as the cover letter, résumé, and mock job interview, are excellent ways of assessing student acquisition and mastery of those profession-specific language skills. Likewise, quizzes can help build student mastery of course content while exams, designed within a significant learning framework as discussed earlier, can demonstrate student mastery not only of content but of overall student learning. Other assignments such as reflection journals and presentations are likewise beneficial in showing not only the formal aspects of student language growth, but also the students' personal growth over the course of the project. In other words, they serve to demonstrate such intangibles as intercultural sensitivity and intercultural competence.

In my experience, assessing project outcomes, including community partnership objectives, is best achieved through observation and the use of formal surveys. All of this serves as documentation that can be used to develop your project, CSL design and its integration into the curriculum, and community partnerships. What your students, the project, the partners, and you collectively produce during the course of the project presents a snapshot that can serve to assess the relative success and potential growth of the project and partnership. Did the project meet its learning and community partner objectives? If not, or even if it did, what needs to be improved or reassessed if the project or community partnership were to be continued? As noted earlier, student learning assessments can provide an overall picture of the project and its impact on the students and community. This, in addition to formal input from community partners and community members, can provide invaluable feedback on the project and partnerships. One way in which to do this is through a survey.

The appendix provides an example of an exit survey that can be used with students, community partners, and community members alike. If applicable to your project, use the survey as a template and guide. In addition, surveys for each respective vested partner can also be produced. Whether surveys are appropriate for your project and whether you choose to engage the community impacted is dependent on the type of project. To the extent possible, however, I encourage that you include direct input from community partners in your final assessment. Considering the challenges involved in designing and implementing CSL in world language higher education, documenting the project and its impact beyond course learning objectives is important for professional development, grant funding, hiring and promotion, and otherwise supporting and validating your interest in and use of CSL as a pedagogical method in world language higher education.

7

Integrating WLSP into Non-WLSP Courses

DEVELOPING AND BRINGING TO fruition an entire course in WLSP may seem a daunting or even impossible task, especially where departmental and other logistical challenges might exist. In such cases, the needs of the teacher, students, and department are better served in adapting and integrating WLSP content and objectives within existing language and culture courses.

Though many undergraduate world language textbooks now include chapters that incorporate WLSP content, there remains a need to more thoroughly integrate WLSP into the higher education world language curriculum beyond the basic language sequence. Indeed, thanks to the communicative method, beginner language textbooks include chapters that teach vocabulary and grammar lessons through such specific learning contexts as the doctor's office, the office space, the airport, and the classroom. While this is a major step in situating vocabulary and grammar within real-world contexts, relegating WLSP to the primary language sequence is yet inadequate for meeting the current standards and needs of higher education world language programs, students, and society. It is therefore imperative that teachers consider integrating WLSP content into courses beyond the primary language sequence, including core intermediate and advanced literature, culture, and language courses. This presents an opportunity to integrate WLSP learning objectives and research and teaching perspectives into world language higher education, regardless of the existence and feasibility of developing WLSP certificates and programs. To this end, this chapter presents practical strategies and models for integrating WLSP into non-WLSP courses based on my experience developing, researching, and teaching topics, lessons, and courses in WLSP. Among the topics discussed are learning objective alignment, lesson planning, classroom activities, and assignment and assessment design.

Curricular Elements
Curriculum design questions for lesson planning in specific courses outside of WLSP are similar to those addressed in WLSP-specific courses. Teachers still need

to think about what the major learning objectives are, how they might build lesson plans, learning activities, and assessments that deliver those objectives, and what resources they need to consider. The only major difference is in thinking about how WLSP content might serve and advance the learning objectives of the course and lesson in question.

At its core, this is an exercise in creative thinking. Rather than question whether WLSP content is suitable, ask *how* it helps deliver the lesson. Might the concerns and issues addressed in medical Spanish be useful in a cultural studies course on the Latinx population in the United States? Might translation and interpreting issues addressed in Spanish for commerce be relevant to a course on literature? How might immigration issues addressed in Spanish for law enforcement be relevant to a Spanish language conversation or composition course? In shifting the emphasis away from vocabulary and grammar acquisition to the core issues, common links can be made across the curriculum. This is not to say that vocabulary and grammar are unimportant, it is simply to resituate them as a means to an end rather than an end in and of themselves.

Learning Objectives

Prior to developing a lesson plan and any activities, assignments, and assessments, give attention to the desired learning objectives. Though the broader course objectives will necessarily differ for each course, within a given lesson there are likely objectives that are shared across courses. This will be the point of entry for integrating WLSP content. Indeed, students are generally expected to identify, explain, and compare and contrast. As the intent of the lesson is to deliver the learning objectives, this presents an opportunity for WLSP content to be integrated in a way that supports and supplements those objectives without compromising the integrity of the lesson, content, and course.

How might WLSP content and perspectives help deliver the lesson objectives? This is the primary question teachers need to consider, regardless of the course, though at first glance some courses and lessons may seem incompatible with WLSP. For example, a course on Spanish composition might have a lesson on register (formal versus informal). The objectives might include the following, in the form of Can-Do statements:

- Students can recognize the difference between formal and informal written registers.
- Students can explain why the need for different registers exists and when it would be appropriate to use one or the other.
- Students can write in and appropriately use formal and informal registers.

In such a lesson, WLSP content from commerce to medicine and just about any other area can be easily integrated as a vehicle for delivering the lesson's objectives. For example, students could learn and practice their formal writing skills through a cover letter and résumé for a job application with a law firm, a major corporation, or an academic position. They could then contrast this with the informal registers they use to write emails, text messages, memes, or other messages they send to their friends or family. Similarly, teachers could ask students to practice their formal and informal writing in designing written content for webpages, brochures, advertisements, grants, legal documents, newspaper articles or op-ed pieces, and political speeches. These could likewise be contrasted with informal registers used in songwriting, journaling, vlogging scripts, and screen plays, for example. In both instances, students learn about and practice writing skills in formal and informal registers while acquiring context-specific vocabulary and preprofessional skills. It also allows for teachers to tap into student personal and professional interests.

At the end of this lesson, students will walk away not only having learned the content, but also with something they can put into their professional portfolio. Indeed, this is, in part, what WLSP proposes, to provide students with learning opportunities that advance student personal, professional, and intellectual growth in situating language use within specific, real-world contexts (Lafford 2012, 2; M. Long 2017a, 3; Sánchez-López 2013a, x). For teachers unaccustomed to deviating from textbook material and creating their own content material, the key is therefore in understanding *how* WLSP content can help deliver the learning objectives of a given lesson. The nuts and bolts of lesson planning as well as specific classroom activities, assignments, and assessments are addressed next.

Lesson Planning

There are several ways in which WLSP can help structure the lesson plan and even course calendar. While a single lesson can be sufficient, sometimes the course and calendar allow for an entire section or module to be aligned with WLSP content. Regardless, the following will briefly describe how language educators might approach a single lesson plan.

Recall that the goal of the lesson is not to teach WLSP content per se, but to deliver the learning objectives. Therefore, you need not stress over whether you have the perceived credentials or qualifications to appropriately "teach" the content material (e.g., medical Spanish, Spanish for law enforcement). Instead, rely upon and build on your strengths and skills as a teacher, as discussed in chapter 3. You know how you best teach. Use this knowledge as your foundation and guide for developing a lesson plan. In a literature and cultural studies course, for example, you might find a mixture of formal presentation, a classroom assignment or activity, and critical discussion useful in helping students to learn the material and concepts. For others, a mixture of experiential activities (e.g., group work, creative writing, and role-playing), audiovisual content (e.g., a documentary film), and critical discussion might feel more comfortable. You may also likely choose to adapt different activities to serve the needs of the lesson at hand. What is most important is to know what works best for you, the students, and the lesson at hand. While the addition of WLSP content does create opportunities for more experiential and reflexive activities in the classroom, it does not mean you have to radically change how you teach. In other words, you are welcome to integrate WLSP content and adapt it to suit your teaching approach, style, and classroom needs, whatever they may be.

Regardless of the preferred method of teaching and classroom activities, a scaffolding approach is recommended to help structure the lesson and student learning.

Though different models of scaffolding exist in education, I use the term here to refer to any teaching methodology that incrementally builds student knowledge in a logical, stepwise, and chaining motion such that by the end of the lesson, students will have fully learned and mastered the skills and concepts. As the literature in education shows, building knowledge in incremental steps helps orient and guide students, providing a framework for integrating new information and building competency in a particular skill area. It also has the added benefit of modeling for students ways of learning and teaching (see Gibbons 2002).

How and where to integrate WLSP into such a framework depends on the extent to which it serves the lesson objectives. If it is intended to be the primary vehicle for teaching the concepts, then it will be fully integrated into the scaffolding framework. If it is meant to deliver one specific point of the lesson's learning objectives (e.g., comparison), then it might be sufficient to integrate it as a single activity. Ultimately, the extent to which you integrate WLSP into the lesson depends on your level of comfort.

For illustration purposes, the appendix includes a sample lesson plan for an advanced Spanish literature course focused on the novel *Love in the Time of Cholera* by Gabriel García Márquez. This lesson plan focuses on the relationships between the main characters as a way of teasing out and commenting on the social, historical, and cultural significance of the book. Given the love triangle between the main characters, a role-playing activity centered round a couple's counseling scenario is featured as the focal point of the lesson. The lesson concludes with a written and comparative reflection that builds on the activity in a way that allows for students to make connections and comparisons.

The sample lesson plan delivers the learning objectives while engaging students with WLSP content. Though somewhat superficial, it nonetheless introduces students to the profession of counseling, specifically couples therapy. It also presents an opportunity to address issues of culture and cultural sensitivity that would likewise factor into counseling. Though not explicitly addressed in the lesson plan, the teacher could integrate cultural issues into the exercise. For example, after talking about different ways that people deal with relationship issues and the profession of couples counseling, the teacher could generate another short discussion about cultural similarities and differences in conceptions of love, gender roles, and societal expectations based on their own backgrounds and understanding of Latin American culture based on the book and other books read in class. The teacher could then ask how cultural differences might impact the choices counselors make with regard to reception, treatment, behavior, questions, expectations, guidelines, feedback, therapy exercises, and assessments. Students might learn, for example, that many in the Latins community turn to family networks and the church for support and guidance and that, though counseling of any sort could benefit many families, such services are only recently being targeted to the Latinx population (see Santiago-Rivera, Arredondo, and Gallardo-Cooper 2002). They might also discuss the fact that there are still many societal expectations in Latin America regarding gender and gender roles and that these can serve as points of contention in a relationship when norms are challenged or fractured in a society with different values, norms, and expectations

(Santiago-Rivera, Arredondo, and Gallardo-Cooper 2002). Though tangential to the book itself, these themes are nonetheless relevant as this fracture in perceptions and expressions of love caused by the collision of the "modern" and "premodern" in Colombia is precisely the context for *Love in the Time of Cholera*. For those students interested in social work, such a discussion reinforces the understanding that perceptions of love, social status, and gender roles and relationships are subjective and that they change with time and place.

Classroom Activities

Classroom activities typically used in non-WLSP courses can readily be adapted to WLSP content. These can include experiential learning activities, writing and conversation activities, group projects, discussion, games, and other activities commonly used in the world language classroom. What is important is not the type of activity, but the way it is structured and used. Just as with the learning objectives, the key is in resourcing the activity in service of the lesson objectives. While the various activities discussed in chapter 4 may also be useful in the non-WLSP classroom, you will necessarily need to tailor the activities to the specific course and learning objectives in question.

Just as in the sample lesson plan discussed earlier, classroom activities need not focus on the teaching of WLSP per se but on helping deliver the objectives by structuring the learning process. There are numerous ways in which this can be done, though more often than not, teachers will find that WLSP-specific activities work well as experiential activities (e.g., group work, role-playing, projects) or conversation and writing exercises. This is because WLSP content, by virtue of its subject, lends itself to practical application. Let us consider three more specific classroom activity examples: a writing and conversation activity, a group activity, and a role-play.

As demonstrated in the earlier lesson plan, a combined writing and conversation activity is a natural way of building on and reinforcing student learning. In the *Love in the Time of Cholera* example, the activity involved students generating scripts that they then practiced and used as guides for improvised dialogues. The same idea and structure can be applied in most any classrooms and with just about any topic and WLSP content area. For example, a lesson plan on race and nation in Latin America for a Latin American studies course on Afro-Latinx populationmight similarly include a writing and conversation activity approached from the perspective of a nongovernmental human rights organization. In such an activity, students would confront the major issues in drafting a proposal for remedying some identified issue (e.g., social equity, access to land, access to education, equal representation) to present before the United Nations. The document would explain the context (what the major issues are) and present possible remedies for addressing those problems. In identifying country or region-specific race-related social issues, the students would also make comparisons with similar issues in other countries in the region and globally. The conversation component would be a presentation to the class (i.e., the "United Nations"), and the class could then vote on the strengths of the proposals (if the teacher so chooses). Such an activity can be done either individually or as a group.

Group-specific activities would similarly include writing and presentation, but the scale of the project would be larger and would give each student an opportunity to complete a specific task. For example, a group classroom activity on writing for journalism might include either small groups or the whole class working as a team to produce a single periodical (magazine, newspaper, or webpage). The students could be given specific tasks (e.g., editor, op-ed writer, advertising, storywriters, news writers). As a part of this assignment, they would need to study relevant periodicals that could serve as models, organize and discuss as a team, write their specific pieces, and put them together using appropriate templates found online or on Microsoft Word or some other word processing or publishing software. Afterword, the groups or class would present and discuss as a class the product and what they learned from the experience. Such an activity could span a single class period or several class periods and would require little input from the teacher.

Role-play is another very common, useful, and engaging classroom activity that allows for the integration of WLSP content and situations. For example, a mock job interview in a conversation course allows students to apply their language skills toward a real-world scenario while the production and performance of a play based on a literary work in a literature, composition, or Latin America studies course likewise exposes students to playwriting, theatre, and the arts in general. Yet another common role-play activity involves interpreting and translation. A Latin American studies course on the Latinx population in the United States might include an interpreting exercise in a medical or legal context. A translation exercise on the same topic might also be useful, especially if students help translate actual brochures, pamphlets, and web content for local organizations and businesses serving the community of the target language.

In addition to being practical and providing exposure to and even training in preprofessional skills, WLSP-related classroom activities provide space for reflection on and discussion of social and cultural issues of relevance. An interpreting exercise, for example, allows students to engage with some of the challenges encountered in a real-life interpreting scenario, whether in a medical, business, legal, political, or other context. In discussing the issues afterword and in further processing through written assignments, such as journals or essays, students are able to personally connect with the issues and themes addressed in class. As this example and that of *Love in the Time of Cholera* show, classroom activities help students become conscious of the issues while follow-up discussion or writing activities allow them to further reflect and process. It is here that students begin to make the connections that lead to the critical thinking and cultural competencies desired in world language classrooms. The assignments and assessments discussed next will help further develop those connections and skills.

Assignments and Assessments

Just as with classroom activities, assignments and assessments can be readily adapted for WLSP content. The purpose in doing so, however, is to deliver and assess mastery of the course and lesson objectives. Journals, research papers, essays, reading summaries and responses, individual and group projects, oral presentations, community service learning projects, and other such assignments currently used in world language classrooms are all suitable for WLSP material. The same is true for formal midterm and final exams, chapter and unit tests, surveys, project and assignment rubrics, and quizzes. Rather than reinvent the wheel, let us consider one specific strategy that you can adapt to your existing assignments and assessments that may prove beneficial, namely adding a reflection component.

As noted, reflection is central to fostering the critical thinking and connections necessary for developing the linguistic and cultural competencies desired in students (see Dantas-Whitney 2002). It is also through this process that the underlying connections between the course and subject material in question and WLSP can be made. In other words, it is the link between theory and practice. Given the opportunities that WLSP topics present for addressing broader social and cultural issues situated in real-world contexts, providing space for reflection in assignments and assessments can only benefit student learning and advance course and world language goals and objectives (e.g., Dantas-Whitney 2002; McBride 2010; Petrov 2013). How reflection might be integrated depends on your level of creativity and comfort, as it presents its own challenges for student assessment. As there are innumerable ways to do so, the following are presented as models and launching points in the development of your own assignments and assessments.

Reflection Writing Assignments

You can readily integrate reflection into almost any writing assignment. A reading guide, for example, can include content questions, comparative questions, and reflection questions. Yet other assignments can be entirely reflection based, such as reflection journals or reading commentaries. Two examples are offered in the appendix: a generic reading guide for *Love in the Time of Cholera* that focuses on the relationship between the main characters and a reflection journal prompt on the same topic.

There are many ways to structure a journal, as discussed in chapter 5, but the key is to use prompts or guidelines that direct students to reflect on and not regurgitate content information. You may need to provide models for your students as reflection writing does not necessarily come naturally to everyone and is indeed a skill that can be developed through practice. Relevant for this chapter is the understanding that reflection questions or prompts differ in scope from other types of questions. Whereas content and comparative questions ask "what, who, where, when, and why," a reflection question typically asks "how." The question "What is the significance of *Love in the Time of Cholera*?" is different from "How is *Love in the Time of Cholera* significant to your life today, if at all?" In answering this question, students may end up answering the what, who, where, and why, but they also go beyond to consider its relevance to their own lives.

The same logic applies to questions in assessments. In addition to content and comparative questions, build space in your tests and exams for questions that allow students to reflect and make broader connections across the course, curriculum, and their own lives and experiences. Just as with the journal prompts, such exam questions ask "how" and would likely be in the form of short essays. Yet another way to do this is through questions that ask students to apply their knowledge and mastery of concepts toward the resolution of a problem or challenge. These sorts of questions are especially useful for testing knowledge and mastery of WLSP content and perspectives. An illustration of this type of question is given in chapter 4, but in the case of a non-WLSP course, the question would necessarily need to be adapted. In keeping with the *Love in the Time of Cholera* example, a test question could ask students to write a counseling scenario with the characters, either a single character, two, or all three in the same session. The question should prompt students to write a script exploring the major themes and issues addressed in class. Though this question is based on the classroom activity, having them produce a new script on their own for the purposes of the exam would demonstrate their knowledge of the book's central characters, themes, issues, and significance, and would likewise demonstrate their mastery of profession-specific vocabulary and issues of cultural sensitivity. As noted previously, the difficulty with such a question, for some, is in its subjectivity. Such an exercise, however, is no less subjective than an essay question. If you are consistent in modeling expectations with such assignments in the classroom, then students should feel comfortable engaging with such a question in an exam. For the purposes of grading, depth of engagement with the subject material in connection with the WLSP-related themes and issues rather than personal opinion takes precedence. A rubric is highly recommended for such questions.

8

Interpreting in WLSP

AS A COMPLEMENT TO existing courses in the world language curriculum on interpreting, this chapter offers practical strategies, exercises, and models in approaching this valuable skill set in WLSP. Differing only in context and approach, the teaching of interpreting in WLSP encompasses both theory and practice, but places even greater emphasis and significance on developing interpreters who are not only proficient in their linguistic abilities and skills but who are aware of and sensitive to the ways in which culture informs the interpretation of meaning. In other words, I teach interpreting in WLSP with the intent to develop and foster among my students cultural awareness, intercultural sensitivity, and competence through greater integration of culture and cultural dynamics in interpreting, as addressed in the previous chapter. Indeed, the importance of how we approach the teaching of these related skills in WLSP cannot be overstated, given the real-world consequences of misinterpreting and translating across languages in such contexts as health care, law enforcement, politics and diplomacy, and commerce. It is here that language proficiency, specific language skills, profession/context-specific knowledge and training, knowledge of other cultures, and intercultural sensitivity and competence intersect, producing empathic and translingual and transcultural competent service providers, professionals, and community members. Given the significance of this topic for WLSP, it can and ought to be implemented in any WLSP course or lesson plan, including those lessons integrated within non-WLSP courses.

Depending on the curricular needs of your program, a specific course in interpreting in WLSP may not be necessary or feasible. That said, it is probable that the demand for change in the higher education world language curriculum drives the need to transform core courses in interpreting from those based on theory to practice. Though knowledge of theory and lexicon are indeed important in the development of competence in interpreting, it is necessary to also consider interpreting from a culture-centered perspective. This chapter takes this understanding as a point of departure for the teaching of interpreting in WLSP. Based on my curriculum development, teaching, and research experience, the following therefore addresses the issue of culture in the teaching of interpreting in WLSP and presents practical strategies, assignments, and models for use in the classroom.

Issues and Strategies

Accuracy, or fidelity of meaning, is perhaps the most significant concern in courses on interpreting taught from any perspective. That said, the context in which and the purposes for which the skills and products of interpreting are applied in WLSP make the task and issue of fidelity that much more imperative and challenging. A misinterpreted or translated phrase may have significant unintended consequences for service providers and the clients or community served. It is not an exaggeration to say that a patient may be misdiagnosed, a transaction opportunity may be missed, a professional relationship may be disrupted, misinformation may be disseminated, and an opportunity to reach an underserved population may be lost. Given the growing need for bilingual service providers and for quality interpreting services, these are not issues to be taken lightly (see Angelelli 2004; Drugan 2017).

Yet, given the linguistic and cultural diversity subsumed within a single language group such as "Spanish," for example, how do we understand and approach the issue of fidelity such that we can ensure that the intentions and needs of organizations, service providers, businesses and the communities they serve are adequately and competently met? What it means is that we must consider, in addition to grammar and theory, extralingual aspects informing meaning production in verbal and written transactions in any given specific context, including culture and nonverbal communication. What it also means is that we must consider intentions. Whom does the service provider, organization, business provider, and so forth desire to serve, and what are the cultural dynamics and factors that need to be considered on the part of the interpreter as a result? The teaching of interpreting in WLSP, therefore, is as much about cultural sensitivity and competence as it is about context-specific knowledge and vocabulary.

Cultural Factors in Interpreting

In interpreting, so many more factors must be taken into consideration than just the words themselves, including cultural and even generational differences in uses of the language and in the meaning of specific words (see Angelelli 2004; Knapp and Hall 2014; Kramsch 1998; Reynolds 2005; Ruggiero 2017a). Culture informs, though not delimits, how we perceive the world around us and how we interact with others as a result (see Kramsch 1998). In the case of WLSP, it also includes how we understand and approach such things as health and wellness, family and community, commerce, the government and law enforcement, and other institutions, professions, and services. It stands to reason that the teaching of WLSP, let alone interpreting in WLSP, take into account culture as a significant component of the process of meaning production in verbal and nonverbal communication (see Angelelli 2004; Ruggiero 2017a).

Let us take for example the Spanish-speaking world. The Spanish predominantly taught in institutions of higher education in the United States is Castilian

Spanish, which originates in the historical Kingdom of Castile, a region that once spanned the northern and central parts of modern day Spain. This stands to reason given the history and diffusion of the Spanish language across the Americas during the colonial period. Yet, the reality is that the language needs of service providers and of Spanish speakers served in the United States in particular are such that the current curricular emphasis on European Spanish leaves those students seeking to serve these communities underprepared and at a disadvantage (see Beaudrie and Fairclough 2012).

In fact, the vast majority of Spanish speakers in the United States prevail from Central America, the Caribbean, and Latin America (Beaudrie and Fairclough 2012, 1). Though mutually intelligible, the Spanish of the different countries constituting the New World are different enough to present challenges to even native speakers, let alone those learning it as a second language. Indeed, in my experience, this is a favorite and inevitable topic of conversation among native Spanish speakers of different countries as well as among heritage learners. A word with a mundane and benign meaning in one country may take on a slanderous and negative connotation in another, making for humorous comparisons and discussions. Even within a given country, variations resulting from exposure and mixture with other languages, including indigenous, creole, and other languages, make for occasional misunderstandings and miscommunication among native Spanish speakers. And then there are those cases in which Spanish cannot be assumed to be the native language of the people of a given region or population (see Leeman 2012). Indeed, in my experience as a medical Spanish interpreter, the assumption that all individuals from a particular country or region share, speak, or even understand the same language is a growing problem for service providers in the United States. If this is the case with the Spanish language and those countries where Spanish is presumed to be the dominant language, it is likely also to be the case with other language areas and those countries with which those languages are associated. All of this is to say that the teaching of interpreting must take into account cultural dynamics and factors in order to better prepare students in service to the professions and to the community.

How, then, do we proceed with the teaching of interpreting beyond the teaching of lexicon and theory? To begin, ask yourself the following questions:

- What community or communities of the target or heritage language are we preparing our students to serve?
- With what community or communities of the target or heritage language are our students likely to be in contact?
- By extension, what culture or cultures are represented within the broader umbrella represented by the target or heritage language?
- What is the linguistic diversity of this population?

Once the target community and language(s) are identified, you will necessarily need to acquaint yourself with the linguistic and cultural nuances that inform language use and meaning production among that population. In Spanish, for example, the Castilian *vosotros* pronoun and verb form, which historically connotes the informal second-person plural, is used predominantly in Spain and only in some variation in the Spanish-speaking Americas. Instead, the formal second-person plural pronoun and verb form of *ustedes* is used in its place. Though Spanish speakers in the Americas will likely have heard and perhaps have studied the Castilian vosotros and would understand its intended meaning, it is probable that some would not know how to form or use it. This means that a teacher might consider developing lessons and assignments for interpreting in WLSP that are reflective of the linguistic nuances of the target or heritage language population served.

In addition to such differences in grammar as pronoun forms and their associated verb conjugations, the diversity of vocabulary and colloquial expressions heard across the Spanish speaking Americas can also be significant. Certain common words, such as "bill," as in an invoice for goods or services, can have many variations, such as *factura*, *cuenta*, and *recibo*. Spanish speakers from different countries may gravitate toward specific words that, though understood across the Spanish-speaking world, may only be used in certain countries. In Argentina, for example, factura is used most frequently to refer to the bill and receipt, while cuenta and recibo are more common in other parts of Latin America. In other instances, words shared across countries may take on different meanings. In Puerto Rico, the word *guagua* means bus while in Ecuador it refers to a baby. Similarly, certain words or expressions may be unique solely to a specific country or region. In the United States, one also finds new words and expressions used among Spanish-speaking immigrants and their descendants. Words such as *roofero* (roofer) and *la troca* (the truck) are used and understood among many Spanish speakers in the United States, though they are not formally taught in schools. Though such colloquial expressions may be taken for granted by Spanish language teachers, for example, it may be that knowledge of such words and expressions may be helpful in interpreting or translating for the local Spanish-speaking population served.

We want to similarly consider the role that culture plays in interpreting (see Angelelli 2004). Knowledge of cultural factors will help shape specific lesson plan activities as well as strategies for teaching interpreting, as addressed later. Within the context of WLSP, you may want to begin by considering the following questions:

- What are the main beliefs or worldviews shared among the target language population?
- How do these beliefs inform the prevailing social values, norms, and customs, including attitudes, behaviors, and social interactions among them?
- How do cultural beliefs and values inform language use and meaning production in a given context, including within the specific context which is the focus of the course or lesson?

In the context of WLSP, these questions and their application in the teaching of interpreting in WLSP take on a practical rather than theoretical function and purpose. Take, for example, the topic of language for health care. Cultural beliefs can make a significant difference in a community's understanding of health and wellness (see Gurung 2014; Joralemon 2017; Winkelman 2009). These can impact how a person and a community understand and respond to a given illness, which in turn affects how they understand and approach treatment options. This could include attitudes toward and uses of traditional and modern Western medicine, the role that family and community play in treatment, and how individuals and communities communicate health needs to medical service providers.

In my experience as a Spanish medical interpreter and Argentine immigrant to the United States, for example, cultural traditions and the family tend to play a central role in the Latinx immigrant and heritage learner understanding and approach to health and health care in the United States. Common ailments and conditions such as indigestion, a cold, aches and pains, and depression might be diagnosed and initially treated via traditional healers or family members versed in the use of medicinal herbs. Faith and the involvement of family in diagnosis, treatment, and care may also be significant in an individual's healing process, reflecting the affective aspects of health and wellness modern Western medicine is now increasingly recognizing. Understanding such factors can make a difference in the outreach efforts of health care service providers, quality and efficacy of the service provided, and in the overall experience for both provider and those individuals and communities served.

Culture also informs nonverbal communication, which can also play a significant role in meaning production. Body language in particular, an area little considered in the literature on interpreting, is especially important to consider in the teaching of interpreting (see Ruggiero 2017a). Hand gestures, body position, posture, gaze, eye contact, facial expressions, touch, and pace of speech can play just as significant a role in meaning production as tone of voice, nonlexical fillers, and other nonverbal forms of communication.

Though it may seem daunting, there are ways to prepare our students to contend with these challenges. Expertise at the level of a sociolinguist or cultural anthropologist is not required. In my experience, it is enough to be aware of the cultural diversity of the community served to begin building lesson plans and exercises that reflect their identity and culture, including their relationship to the target language. Raising awareness of the role that culture plays in communication and interpreting likewise goes a long way toward developing student intercultural sensitivity and competence, as addressed in the previous chapter.

Interpreting Assignment and Model

The interpreter dialogue included in chapter 4 is excellent for helping students learn how to do simultaneous interpreting within any specific context. For convenience, a blank template is provided in the appendix. Though the assignment may at first involve translation, it can be used as a basis for a simultaneous interpreting exercise.

The interpreting exercise may be assigned in stages. After providing students with the context and relevant input (e.g., vocabulary and cultural considerations), you may ask students to write a script, complete with dialogue in the target language of the respective speakers and the accompanying translation (English to target language and vice versa). This allows students to practice language composition and translation skills as well a s to generally see how the interpreting scenario might be enacted. It also provides them with a structure for an actual interpreting scenario. Alternately, the interpreter assignment may also be created in class in groups of two or three students. In both instances, students may perform the scripted interpreting scenario for their peers for comparative purposes. Discussion of interpreter choices in translation may follow.

In addition to scripting an interpreter dialogue, the instructor may ask students to perform an impromptu simultaneous interpretation. This may follow the original script worked on by the students. In such case, the individual performing the role of the interpreter would render a simultaneous interpretation based on the original scripted dialogue but without reference to the written translation. Likewise, and for more advanced language students, the interpreting scenario may involve an entirely improvised dialogue based on the original subject matter, characters, and cultural parameters of the assignment. In this instance, the student serving as the interpreter would perform an actual, spontaneous simultaneous interpretation, such as would be expected in a real-world professional context. In all instances, critical class discussion of the student-interpreted dialogues facilitated by the instructor would follow. Such a discussion would focus on interpreter choices and cultural and other factors informing the interpretation. In this way, students learn the relevant language and interpreting skills through practice and discussion as well as gain exposure to key issues in simultaneous interpreting.

Yet another consideration in the teaching of interpreting beyond the development of professional language skills is the relevance of body language for the interpreter. Academic preparation in nonverbal communication, from a behavioral science and communication studies perspective, is not necessary for such an assignment, though it may be informative for you as a teacher. Suffice it to say that interpreting meaning in verbal communication without reference to body language can be challenging, and this basic fact can be a starting point for critical observation and conversation among students.

As a preliminary discussion, ask your students to come up with examples of instances of miscommunication where the interpretation of meaning has been misunderstood between themselves and their friend or families. Students might mention text messages, emails, and possibly even phone conversations. Ask them to reflect on why this might be. Eventually, they should note the lack of nonverbal cues, including body language. What body language and other nonverbals do they use to express meaning? Have them give specific examples. Then ask whether the ways in which they express themselves nonverbally are universal. After the discussion, you can provide specific examples of culture-specific nonverbal cues to demonstrate differences in nonverbal communication. Then provide students with examples of relevance specific to the target language in question. In a Japanese business language course, for example, business etiquette extends beyond language to include nonverbals, including bowing, eye-contact, and ways of presenting gifts and items such as business cards. Whenever possible, play audio-visual examples of interpersonal communication that shows cultural patterns in nonverbal communication. Lastly, ask your students to consider what role cultural differences in body language and nonverbals play in simultaneous interpreting. What factors might an interpreter have to take into consideration? How might this inform interpreter choices?

To put this into practice, students might practice interpreting in the formation of a triangle. Rather than having the interpreter stand beside either the service provider/caregiver or the client/patient, position them between them such that they form a triangle. This formation in simultaneous interpreting facilitates communication in that it allows for direct eye contact and for the interpretation of body language and other nonverbals. When using this body positioning formation in combination with the earlier interpreting exercise, it is recommended that students playing the role of the interpreter use the first-person in interpreting and instruct the parties involved to direct their gaze toward one another as they speak, rather than toward the interpreter. In the post-interpreting-exercise discussion, students may also, therefore, address how nonverbal communication and cultural differences in nonverbals inform the interpretation of meaning in a professional interpreting context.

9

Culture and WLSP

THIS CHAPTER IS ABOUT how to approach and integrate culture into the teaching of WLSP. Language is culture, and thus we can understand culture as the core of world language education, whether through the lens or context of literature, linguistics, cultural studies, or WLSP (Brown 2000). The current push in higher education toward applied programs of study, of which the growth of WLSP is a part, may seem like a move away from the humanities and therefore from culture, but nothing could be further from the truth. Without culture, there can be no interpretation of meaning; there can be no communication, in short. You cannot teach world languages without teaching culture and vice versa. There is no need, therefore, to debate the place of culture in any language course because it simply is implied in the subject. Furthermore, an emphasis on culture integrated with language and community is integral to fostering intercultural sensitivity and competence and is therefore also consistent with the teaching objectives of WLSP in world language higher education (see Byram 1997; Byram and Feng 2004; Kim 2020; Ruggiero 2018a).

That said, the current and artificial division between those who study and teach languages from a humanities perspective versus those who do so from an applied one makes this chapter a necessity for those who wish to teach WLSP. This chapter, therefore, serves as a bridge and as an invitation to those in cultural studies or literature who are uncertain as to how business languages and medical interpreting, for example, might be relevant to their existing courses and how those subjects might be taught from a more culture-oriented focus. Based on my experience teaching and developing culture-centered courses and lessons in WLSP, the following presents practical advice, activities, and models for teachers hoping to integrate WLSP subjects into their existing coursework as well as develop WLSP courses from a culture- and humanities-oriented perspective.

Strategies in Integrating WLSP from a Culture-Centered Perspective

The applied aspects of WLSP are often foregrounded in the teaching and research of the subject. While this is an important and integral part of WLSP, this tendency leads to the perception that WLSP is somehow antithetical to a humanities and therefore culture-centered and critical approach. It also leads to the erroneous perception that teachers with literature and cultural studies backgrounds who lack expertise in an applied area of language study are unable to teach WLSP. Nothing could be further from the truth. Indeed, the fact that culture is at the core of all communication, and therefore language study, is all that is needed to rectify this problem. In short, WLSP *is* culture.

Taking culture as the core of WLSP study and teaching, educators across the fields of linguistics, literature, and cultural studies can approach and integrate WLSP into their courses on equal footing. The teaching of WLSP becomes less about the content, per se, than it does about the perspective that the teacher is able to bring to bear on the topic. What this means is that no two teachers will necessarily teach the same WLSP topic in the same way, and this is OK precisely because it means that teachers are building on their own respective strengths in developing their courses, lesson plans, and activities.

A teacher with an interest in film studies, for example, might consider how to incorporate film into the teaching of WLSP and, by extension, include classroom activities and assignments that provide critical perspectives on culture. Yet another teacher with a focus on Latin American literature and culture might find a way to combine an interest in magical realism with a lesson on business languages and culture in Latin America, especially around the concepts of time and relationships. How, exactly, depends largely on the flexibility and creativity of the individual in question, but there are a few questions teachers may want to consider as a starting point:

- What are my strengths and interests as a teacher and as a person?
- What are my interests in WLSP? What calls my attention?
- What WLSP topics might be of relevance to my courses and lesson plans?
- How might I combine my personal strengths and interests with the teaching of WLSP topics?
- How might students benefit from culture-centered WLSP lessons or activities in my courses?

These questions are intended as a point of departure for designing creative and inventive lesson plans and activities. Indeed, the questions are similar to the ones noted in the beginning of the book, but they differ with respect to context. Once teachers have made the decision to adopt WLSP into their existing courses, integration is a matter of understanding how the topics and materials serve the needs, perspective, and objectives of the teacher, course, and lesson plan. To that end, the following section presents sample activities that can serve as models and practical guides.

Models and Activities

One of the challenges in integrating culture in any introductory language classroom is the matter of expertise and lack of cultural knowledge on the part of teachers and students alike. Just as in the fear of approaching WLSP for lack of professional background experience and knowledge, the reluctance to engage matters of culture, including social and historical issues of relevance, is often the result of a perceived lack of cultural knowledge and sensitivity. Teachers may tend to homogenize cultural differences within a language area while outsourcing the culture component of class-room instruction to course materials such as textbooks and audiovisuals. Likewise, students might choose not to engage in discussion for fear of being wrong or singled out for being ignorant at best or insensitive at worst. One of the main ways in which this tendency can be mitigated is through open and transparent dialogue about the limits of knowledge and the nature of the learning process.

Metacognitive activities and exercises go a long way toward alleviating the fear and weight of expertise that prevents meaningful discussions around culture to take place in the classroom. Metacognition refers to inquiry into the learning process itself (see Anderson 2002; Haukås 2018). As a pedagogical method, it can take the form of any learning activity that allows students to ask questions of the language learning process, such as the following:

- How is a language learned?
- How is learning a second language different from learning a heritage language?
- How is communication and meaning negotiated in the language learning process?
- What role does language play in the negotiation of meaning within specific cultural contexts, including the professions and the community, as well as across cultures?
- What role does culture play in the construction and negotiation of meaning in language, and what is the relationship of culture to learning a second or heritage language?
- What is my language learning process, and how might reflection on the ques-tions above benefit my language learning abilities?

The goal is to empower students to develop strategies for language learning and communication across languages, cultures, and specific contexts by helping them to become aware of the language learning process and its issues, including the role that culture plays in language learning and the production and negotiation of meaning in communication. Metacognitive exercises can include journal and other reflection assignments, experiential activities such as singing and dancing, role-playing, and CSL, critical analysis of cultural texts such as film and poetry, and classroom discus-sion, among others. Reflection is key, however, as this allows students to explore, bridge, and integrate how they best learn with how language learning is currently understood and approached in the classroom and in real-world, specific social and cultural contexts, including in the professions and community.

Songs or other forms of oral poetry, for example, can be used as a basis for teaching about and reflecting on culture as well as on the language learning process in general within WLSP. A course on Spanish for health and health care might include a lesson plan on traditional medicine and medical practices in Latin America. Traditional medicine in Latin America is typically holistic, integrating various aspects of culture, from complex cultural belief systems, ritual performances, material culture, kinship networks, music, dance, the visual arts, performance, food and drink, herbs, and nature in the treatment of an individual. Song in particular is often used for therapeutic purposes, whether by specialists or by the afflicted individuals themselves. In such an instance, the teacher might teach a song or rhyme like *sana que sana* (heal, heal) to introduce discussion of culture and its role in different approaches to health and wellness in Latin America. A well-known children's song, "Sana que sana" is about a little frog whose tail is in need of healing:

Sana que sana
Colita de rana
Si no sanas hoy
Sanaras mañana

Heal, heal,
Little frog tail
If you do not heal today
You will heal tomorrow

Though not used to effect healing, per se, the song speaks to the use of music as a therapeutic and didactic purpose among children in Latin America. The song teaches children that the body is capable of healing itself, and thus helps to comfort and reassure them when facing such common injuries as cuts, scrapes, and bruises. It also speaks to the close connection traditional medicine and many cultures in Latin America generally have with nature in that the natural world serves as a teacher and guide, especially where health and wellness are concerned. Lastly, the song serves as a vehicle for transmission of cultural knowledge, thus teaching children about the value of expressive culture as a means of encoding and transmitting culture as well as of affecting healing through not only the song text but also through the joy of song and dance. After teaching the song, the teacher might ask students to interpret the song and generate a reflexive discussion, providing context along the way. Teachers might ask questions such as the following:

- What does this song teach children about healing?
- What does it say about the relationship between nature and cultural conceptions of bodily healing?
- How might this song be used to help a child to feel better when ill or hurt?
- What role can you surmise song and nature play in healing in Latin America?
- What role does song and other oral traditions play in transmitting cultural knowledge?

- What role does language play in all of this?
- Do you know of any songs from your culture that relate to health and healing or that perform a similar function?

From here, the teacher can proceed with the lesson plan, which might include a formal presentation on traditional medicine in Latin America and an experiential activity such as an interpreting role-play, as suggested in the previous chapter, or a composition assignment and concluding reflexive discussion on the challenges in providing medical services in cross-cultural health care settings. In such a lesson, culture plays a central role in Spanish for health care, and the primary WLSP component would revolve around the intersection between traditional and modern Western medicine.

The World Café method is yet another metacognitive, discussion based reflection activity that is most useful for helping teachers and students "break the ice," so to speak, and allow meaningful integration of culture in a WLSP classroom or lesson context, regardless of the classroom and context.[1] Developed in the 1990s in California by a group of concerned individuals representing the spectrum of the community, from higher education to politics and commerce, the World Café is designed to facilitate meaningful dialogue around issues of relevance among diverse participants with the end of generating creative solutions. Held in a café-like ambience created by the facilitator, the method involves small group discussions on a series of related questions that are led by table leaders. Participants, other than the table leaders, change tables for every question, thus maximizing the number of different people, perspectives, and ideas with which they engage during the session. Every table is equipped with a large pad of paper, pens, markers, post-it notes, and other related writing materials. Participants are free to discuss, draw, doodle, and otherwise record their thoughts on the large pad of paper. This paper stays on the table with the table leader and thus represents the sum total of ideas recorded on the paper generated by the group at that particular table. At the end of the small group discussion there is what is referred to as a "harvest," in which table leaders share the ideas generated by the group. Though the method is standardized and is originally intended for use broadly outside of the context of academia, it may likewise be adapted for use in educational settings.

Within the context of a WLSP lesson or classroom, the World Café may be used to address broader questions and issues of culture otherwise overshadowed by lexical concerns. The appendix includes a specific lesson plan and sample World Café exercise created for a Spanish for commerce lesson taught in an advanced Spanish language course. Depending on the needs of the course, instructor, and students, teachers may choose to integrate the World Café discussion either at the beginning or the end of modules or units. For the purposes of this chapter, however, the lesson plan included in the appendix is designed in two parts: the teaching and learning of the content and the discussion activity. While the discussion surrounding culture is foregrounded in the World Café, it is also integrated into the teaching of the content. The difference, however, is that the discussion activity allows for students to make bridges between the materials, how they and other students understand the questions and issues, and how they and other students relate their understanding of culture to the content of the lesson itself.

Other ways of integrating culture into the teaching of WLSP include orienting lesson plans to tell a story. In other words, the content itself is taught in such a way as to convey a particular idea about culture. This is similar to the communicative approach in the sense that grammar and vocabulary serve a higher purpose. For example, the first part of the lesson plan referred to earlier and included in the appendix situates the teaching of the relevant vocabulary and grammar within a specific cultural context. As the teacher presents the input material and moves through the lesson, the students not only learn the content, but are also exposed to key cultural ideas and issues that can be used for further reflection activities and assignments such as the World Café or journals.

Specific activities and assignments may similarly be designed in such a way as to contextualize the content material. The interpreting assignment and template introduced in chapter 4 and provided in the appendix suffice to demonstrate how this might look. The interpreting exercise situates students in different roles within a medical Spanish context: the doctor, the interpreter, and the student. When students write and role-play the assignment, they are exposed to and practice the relevant content and professional skills as well as cultural issues that may factor into the process of interpreting. A follow up reflection activity, such as a written assignment, journal, or discussion facilitated by the instructor, would suffice to tease out the ways in which culture is included in this exercise.

In addition to the two specific metacognitive discussion-based examples given earlier, there are innumerable ways in which culture can be worked into WLSP lesson plans. Integrating song and dance, visual arts, technology, film, and material culture are some of the more obvious ways of doing so, around which activities and discussion can be generated. Indeed, film is treated in a separate chapter in this book, given the relative ease of accessibility of non-English films through platforms such as Netflix and even YouTube. Yet, as argued at the outset of this chapter, even the seemingly mundane use of language within specific contexts, such as the professions, provides opportunity for critical discussion of culture as they reveal particular discourses informed by time and place. In short, to teach WLSP *is* to teach culture, and teachers ought to take seriously the notion that the teaching of WLSP is no different than any other language subject in this regard.

Note

1.   For more information on the World Café history, design, and method, see the following website: http://www.theworldcafe.com/.

10

Heritage Language Learners and WLSP

THIS CHAPTER IS ABOUT approaching heritage language learner, often referred to as heritage learner (HL) education in WLSP. The term heritage learners (HLs) refers to students who are studying a language they have been exposed to by virtue of birthright, regardless of proficiency (see Beaudrie and Fairclough 2012; Zapata and Lacorte 2018b). The growing number of HLs, in the United States in particular, has led language educators to consider the needs and implications of this population for world language education (e.g., Beaudrie and Fairclough 2012; Beaudrie, Ducar, and Potowski 2014; King de Ramírez 2016, 2017; Ruggiero 2017b, 2017c, 2019b; Zapata and Lacorte 2018b). What we as language educators are now beginning to realize is that HLs present a unique opportunity to rethink the "what," "how," and "why" of the WL curriculum. Specifically, it forces us to consider how HL engagement with language study impacts not only HL language development, but also identity formation, sense of self-worth and value, and the local and global economy and communities of the target language. Language educators across the curriculum and in WLSP in particular are poised to make a significant contribution to HL education in the twenty-first century. They are key to bridging language, culture, and community and developing curricula in WLSP and world languages that are responsive to HL needs, backgrounds, and potential contributions. To this end, the following considers issues in HL education in WLSP and presents teaching strategies for world language educators of all backgrounds based on my curriculum development, teaching, and research experience in the areas of WLSP and HLs.

Issues

HLs are a unique learning population within WLSP and WL education with special educational needs and trajectories (King de Ramírez 2017, 55). Specifically, they are distinct from L2 learners in their relationship to their respective heritage language(s), culture(s), and local communities of the heritage language. They are also unique in terms of their diverse cultural and ethnic/racial makeup and backgrounds; upbringings; immigration, social, and economic backgrounds and experiences; and educational and career interests and prospects. These differences need to be taken into account when developing curricula, especially at institutions and programs where there are significant HL populations (see Zapata and Lacorte 2018a, 8).

Diversity in cultural backgrounds and language proficiency among HLs is perhaps the most pressing problem for language teachers (Zapata and Lacorte 2018a, 9). Within the US Spanish HL population, these differences pose a particular challenge for WL educators in terms of course and level placement, choice of teaching strategies and materials, and assessment. In my experience, a mixed HL and L2 classroom can pose benefits for both groups of learners. It can also place a burden on teachers to develop and deliver two separate sets of lesson plans and instructional materials. For this reason, separate courses and even programs for HLs are beginning to emerge (see Luo, Li, and Li 2019). This issue is just as relevant for WLSP course, program, and lesson development, especially when considering course content and teaching strategies (see King de Ramírez 2017; Zapata and Lacorte 2018b). Lending to these challenge is the diversity of HL social and cultural backgrounds, experiences, and motivations. These differences can inform language use and proficiency, cultural knowledge, motivation for language learning, and educational and career interests and goals (King de Ramírez 2017; Zapata and Lacorte 2018b). Yet, while these may pose a challenge for teachers in a mixed HL and L2 classroom, they also present a unique opportunity for attending to the affective domains of language learning.

There is indeed an opportunity in WL higher education and in the world of WLSP to strengthen HL language skills while validating and empowering them to realize their potential as students, professionals, members of local and global communities, and individuals. Yet, how should this be done in the context of WLSP, where so much emphasis is placed on the development of professional language skills? The key to answering this question lies in recognizing the value of HLs in terms of their respective backgrounds, cultural knowledge, and language abilities (King de Ramirez 2017, 56). This perspective reflects an assets-based approach to HLs, which seeks to leverage HL abilities in the design and delivery of courses geared toward their particular strengths and needs (e.g., King de Ramírez 2017; Martínez and Schwartz 2012; Petrov 2013; Ruggiero 2019b). As the scholarship shows, HLs contribute to the learning environment, whether in a mixed HL and L2 classroom or not, with their perspective on language and culture in specific contexts (e.g., Beaudrie, Ducar, and Potowski 2014; Carreira and Kagan 2011; Wong and Xiao 2010; Wu, Lee, and Leung 2014; Zapata 2018). This presents great opportunities for teachers, through reflection assignments like journals and portfolios, classroom discussion, and service learning projects, to advance the following:

- Professional language development and preprofessional skills
- Knowledge of cultural similarities and differences within and across the heritage language and heritage language community
- Knowledge of broader social and cultural issues affecting the heritage language community in the professional workplace and community
- Personal relationships to these issues and the heritage language community

This goes a long way toward strengthening HL self-esteem, cultural identity, and relationship to the heritage language community, thereby attending to the affective domains of WL and WLSP education (see King de Ramírez 2016, 2017; Ruggiero 2017b, 2019b). Indeed, HLs, along with field of WLSP, are showing the way forward as to how to begin developing a higher education world language curricula that is responsive to the needs of our students and community. Next are specific strategies for approaching WLSP education for HLs based on the their particular needs and the challenges and opportunities they present, as demonstrated in my teaching and curriculum development experience as well as in current best practices in HL education in WLSP.

Strategies

Regardless of topic and students, teachers want to be flexible and adapt to the specific strengths and backgrounds of their students. This is especially true, however, in working with HLs. Focus on bringing out from HLs their personal stories and connections with the language and culture that make language learning and interest in WLSP and their respective career choices meaningful. In short, empower HLs through course materials, assignments, and activities that encourage reflection. What is so special, however, about WLSP topics and courses for HLs, in comparison to other lessons and courses in world languages, is that they allow HLs to see themselves as professionals in a society that often sees them as a problem rather than as part of the solution. The following three activities provide instructors a template and basic strategies for how to approach HLs in a WLSP course or lesson.

The HL interpreting exercise included in the appendix is designed for a mixed HL and L2 classroom. As discussed in the chapter on interpreting, students have the opportunity to interpret a dialogue based on a script that can be assigned beforehand. When performed in class, the students are placed in groups of three, ideally mixing the HLs amongst the groups so that each group has at least one HL. This helps to empower HLs by placing them in a productive position as peer tutors among their L2 classmates. It also helps to balance performance and fluency skills in the interpreting assignment, so that students may see variations in language use modeled in the classroom during the impromptu interpreting activity based on scripted dialogue. In the case of the HLs, greater emphasis in assessment is placed on fluency of conversation, rather than fidelity of translation per se. In other words, teachers should play to the strengths of the HLs and use the linguistic variance of HLs to help the students learn about cultural differences in language use and issues in interpreting meaning across languages. In terms of culture, reflection afterward regarding HL experiences with interpreting may likewise prove insightful for the class, given the experience many HLs have with interpreting and translating for their own respective families.

The second HL activity included in the appendix is a résumé and narrative cover letter assignment that encourages students to consider career choices and issues of cultural representation. Teachers may begin by exploring representations of members of the HL community in the profession in question. For example, if discussing

Latinx medical professionals, an instructor might use popular TV dramas such as ER, Chicago MD, and The Good Doctor to illustrate and raise questions for discussion about the representation of Latinx medical professionals:

- Are Latinx medical professionals represented?
- To what extent and in what capacity?
- How are they represented or portrayed?
- What issues (e.g., stereotypes, problems, needs) are raised in these characters and scenarios?
- To what extent do they represent the actual cultures, languages, history, and social and health issues and needs of the Latinx population in the United States today?

The second part of the assignment consists of further reflection in the form of writing or discussion (depending on the needs of the course). The primary question students want to address in this section is whether they have considered entering into that profession:

- Have you considered being a medical doctor, a surgeon, a nurse, a first responder, or an administrator within the health industry?
- How are these ambitions or career paths informed by social, cultural, and family dynamics?
- What advantages and benefits might there be for HLs to become involved in these professions for the self, the profession, and the community?

In the final part of the assignment, students are asked to write a résumé and narrative cover letter for a position in that field showcasing their strengths, skills, and thoughts regarding their potential value to the profession. This allows HLs to not only see themselves in these professional fields and positions, but to consider what strengths and benefits their cultural backgrounds and language skills have for the field and community.

Lastly, CSL is an excellent way of connecting classroom learning with the community and real-world applications and needs. For HLs, this becomes even more significant as they begin to see themselves as positive role models and agents for social change in the heritage language community. Just as with the other activities, CSL design for HLs differs from that for the L2 population only in terms of emphasis. Learning objectives, for example, need not change, only shift from an emphasis on proficiency to fluency and intercultural competence. Flexibility in terms of the depth of involvement will also likely differ, as HLs may be able to help organizations and engage with the heritage language community in ways L2 learners may not otherwise be able to. Beyond language acquisition and preprofessional training, the goal of CSL for HLs is to expose them to cultural diversity within the heritage language community and to social and cultural issues of relevance, strengthen their identity and connection with the heritage language community, and empower them to make a difference through their chosen career paths and connection with their cultural heritage and identity. The primary way to do this is through frequent reflection over the duration of a project in the form of journals, portfolio assignments, discussion, presentations, and formal writing assignments (e.g., comparative and reflection essays). General issues and questions to consider at the outset of HL CSL project design in WLSP include, but are not limited to, the following:

- What language abilities and cultural knowledge do HLs bring to the project, community partners, and community?
- How can the project in question be designed so as to best leverage HL language abilities and cultural knowledge in service to the partner, community, and course objectives?
- In what capacity might HLs serve?
- How might the project be designed such that HLs are exposed to a broad or diverse population in the target language or segment of the community in general?
- What opportunities do they have to reflect on their cultural heritage and language abilities?
- What social issues and cultural issues within the community and professional area are the HLs being exposed in this project? How might these issues be foregrounded in project assignments so as to help HLs reflect on issues of relevance to identity formation, the profession, and the community?

Flexibility in project design is key in helping HLs in particular maximize their CSL experience. Teachers should encourage HLs to assist in the design of the learning and service objectives, thus allowing the students to tailor the project to their own interests, strengths, backgrounds, and needs. As with the other projects, however, providing space for reflection is necessary for them to bridge the classroom and community as well as the project and course with their cultural heritage and career interests.

11

Communication Technology, WLSP, and CSL in the Wake of COVID-19

THIS CHAPTER CONCERNS THE significance of communication technology and the relevance of WLSP and CSL in addressing pedagogical challenges and engaged scholarship responses to public health and natural disaster crises. In the wake of the COVID-19 pandemic and the growing frequency of weather-related catastrophes, such as Hurricane Katrina, world language educators as well as other academics and institutions of higher learning are increasingly called upon to assist with national and local aid and other relief mobilizations. Immigrant and other underserved communities are often hit hardest by such disasters in terms of the economic, health-related, educational, and broader social impact. Though COVID-19 is a distinctly new challenge for humanity, it has thus far proven no different in terms of how it is affecting immigrant, heritage language, and other underserved populations around the world. This reality puts into relief the necessity, value, and relevance of WLSP for world language higher education, engaged scholarship, and society as a whole.

Despite the challenges that COVID-19 and social distancing measures in particular pose to education and traditional outreach efforts, communication technology, in part, is being adapted by teachers and institutions to address the needs of students and local communities. Though the future is uncertain as to the use of and necessity for social distancing measures as a public health intervention, this experience nonetheless presents an opportunity to rethink traditional paradigms and models of education and community engagement, as will most certainly be borne out in the scholarship to follow this pandemic. How we understand community, for example, in light of social distancing and the role that communication technology is currently playing in extending that concept beyond physical boundaries will come to inform how we teach WLSP, approach CSL, and provide needed community outreach during times of crisis for a long time to come. This chapter therefore complements the information contained in the previous chapters, in particular those relating to CSL, and serves to further reinforce the significance and relevance of WLSP for world language higher education in the twenty-first century. Presented next are strategies and ideas for approaching the teaching of WLSP in the context of remote learning and for the development and implementation of CSL with the aid of communication technology.

Distance Learning and WLSP Pedagogy

We are in an age where distance learning technology and remote instruction are highly prioritized and sought after by institutions and students alike. This is even more so the case following social distancing measures initiated in light of COVID-19. While this is not a solution to the current educational challenges in terms of updating pedagogy, diversifying classrooms, defraying tuition costs, and making accessible higher education, it is nonetheless a significant response that has allowed millions of students to continue their education, teachers to retain their jobs, institutions to keep their doors open, and community partners to accomplish their objectives. Long after COVID-19 and social distancing, distance learning will be a part of the fabric of higher education for the foreseeable future.

Beyond the question of tools and strategies, what are the possibilities, limitations, and implications of remote learning for WLSP? To date, there exist no known studies of WLSP distance learning and only two addressing communication technology in remote service-learning projects in WLSP (King de Ramírez 2016; Ruggiero and Hill 2016). This means that there is limited or tangential data to address these questions beyond circumspection. More studies are certain to follow, however, in the wake of social distancing. Suffice it to say that remote learning is about more than integrating new technology. What is most important, as stressed in this book, is an overall emphasis on instructional design.

Though the same can be said for CSL project design in WLSP courses, more can be said about the benefits and implications of integrating communication technology in WLSP service-learning projects. In partnership with the campus radio station and with input from the local Latinx community, King de de Ramírez (2016) had students in a traditional classroom environment develop Spanish-language radio program content addressing topics of relevance for the Spanish-speaking population on and off campus. Likewise, Ruggiero and Hill (2016) used online communication technology, including collaborative tools such as Google Drive, to connect students in a rural high school in Michigan with a nonprofit organization, Global Brigades, providing outreach services to communities in Honduras. Just as in a traditional CSL project where students engage face-to-face with a local community of the target language, the projects in King de Ramírez (2016) and Ruggiero and Hill's (2016) studies saw benefits for student development of specialized language and preprofessional skills, and intercultural sensitivity and competence. In addition, the projects likewise met the objectives of community partners and the communities served. Specific design aspects of both projects will be considered later. The greater implication of these studies, however, has to do with our conception of community and how we deliver service-learning to communities of the target language.

These studies show us that our definition of community can be broadened to include (1) the campus community, (2) nonlocal communities of the target language, and (3) the global target-language community. By extension, the same can be said about community partners (e.g., transnational nongovernmental organizations like the World Health Organization, as opposed to local community organizations). By broadening the scope of what we mean by community in such cases, the concept of service-learning is also extended to include interpersonal communication facilitated by communication technology. Strategies for how to do so more effectively are considered next. What this means for WLSP is that there is great potential for bridging an evident service gap in extending much needed outreach to communities of the target language that might not otherwise be reached due to such extreme measures as social distancing.

Developing and Implementing Virtual CSL Projects in WLSP

Communication technology and emerging social media platforms and tools make possible the extension of CSL beyond traditional models of community engagement. Remote CSL projects can be integrated into WLSP whether the class be traditional, hybrid, or online. How you design and integrate your project, what online platforms and tools you use, and the extent to which students engage with community partners and the community of the target language depends on the resources available, including partners and technology, and on the shared objectives of the project. Regardless of the decisions made, there are a few factors to take into consideration that can help with maximizing the benefits of virtual CSL for students, teachers, partners, and communities alike.

The first step in developing a virtual CSL project is assessing the resources at your disposal, from potential partners to technological support. Just as in a traditional CSL project, you want to consider the following questions:

- What past or current local community partners provide virtual outreach to communities in the target language?
- What opportunities are there to partner with a transnational organization or company providing service to target language communities, whether locally, nationally, or abroad? Consider networking through current study abroad and international programs through your institution.
- How is community outreach currently being delivered by those partners identified? What technology is being used? How effective is the outreach? How might a partnering enhance the quality of outreach and service delivered to the communities affected?
- What technological support does your institution provide? Is there a campus radio station or radio, television, and film program students might be able to partner with? Are there students, faculty, or programs in technology on campus that might be able to provide support, assistance, or partnerships? What audio-visual equipment might be available to students?
- What strengths, professional skills, interests, and technological skills do your students bring that might be beneficial to community partners? Keep in mind that many of today's students bring a level of ease with technology, especially in the area of social media, that can be readily resourced in the context of virtual CSL to enhance student learning and benefit partners and the community.

There are many organizations, institutions, and businesses that provide virtual support to communities all over the world. This was the case prior to the COVID-19 pandemic but is now especially so following the implementation of social distancing measures. Engaging with a partner with an existing online presence and outreach agenda is perhaps most beneficial, as you can then develop a project that provides immediate support in a meaningful and beneficial way to the partner(s) and community in question. If no such outreach is currently being provided by the partner(s) or if you and the partner(s) decide to collaborate on a new project, than a needs assessment can help determine the scope and aims of the project itself. In all instances, collaboration between the teacher, partner(s), and community will help determine the shared objectives and the degree and type of student involvement.

Just as in the case with traditional face-to-face CSL projects, designing virtual service-learning projects for WLSP requires equitable collaboration and an alignment of objectives. Experience shows that input from all vested parties, including students, will help ensure that all objectives are met, including learning objectives, and that projects are equitable (see Ruggiero 2018c). Where and when possible, input on the part of the community (e.g., community members), and not just the partner(s), is important in the development of a CSL project, as it ensures the support and engagement of the community. This is significant in defining outcomes that are meaningful to the community in question and in measuring the relative success of a given project. Where the community is more broadly defined as a result of the scope of the project (e.g., a national, international, or global project), "community" input will necessarily be discerned from an assessment of needs as identified through scholarly and partner research. If the purpose of academic community engagement is to empower and build capacity among those communities most affected by social and economic inequity, than it stands to reason their voices must also be included in the decision making process.

Apart from the technology and tools used to facilitate the project, the process of designing, integrating, and assessing the project and outcomes is no different than that involved in traditional CSL. These steps are considered in the previous chapters of this book on CSL in WLSP. Suffice it to say that an alignment of objectives along with equitable circumstances, including ample collaboration between vested parties, and a balanced classroom and service learning experience will go a long way toward ensuring a successful CSL project. Whether virtual or traditional, CSL provides world language students in a WLSP context with ample opportunity to develop specific language skills, cultural knowledge, intercultural competence, and preprofessional skills. In addition, exposing students to the broader social, economic, historical, and political context affecting the daily lives of the target language community in question, whether locally, nationally, or globally, helps students to further develop empathy and compassion for others. Though intercultural sensitivity is often measured in the context of traditional interpersonal communication in cross-cultural contexts (see Bennett 1993), the research that is certain to follow on virtual CSL will likely suggest that this is also the case as a result of intercultural exposure and interaction online. Foregrounding this aspect of CSL is important in keeping with the broader social objectives of WLSP and world language pedagogy.

Though few models exist for virtual CSL projects, the following suggestions are provided as a starting point for imagining the different types of projects that might be beneficial for community partners regardless of their location:

- Developing podcast episodes of relevance to partners and the community
- Developing blogs or vlogs (video logs) of relevance
- Producing relevant online content for partner websites and social media platforms
- Translating online content for partners
- Providing simultaneous interpreting services using platforms such as Zoom, Google Meet, or other teleconferencing apps
- Providing relevant culture and demographics research for partners developing existing or new outreach programs
- Developing and facilitating online discussion forums, roundtables, or community conversations around topics of relevance (e.g., issues such as health, immigration, or education) using online platforms such as Zoom or Google Meet
- Facilitating project development or partner virtual communications needs using shared documents like Google Docs

As communication technology and social media platforms advance for virtual and long-distance communication, so to shall the myriad ways in which institutions of higher education and scholars engage with local and global communities. In their essence, however, CSL and other forms of community-based education will remain the same, as will how you integrate them within your existing teaching experience, classroom needs, agenda, and learning outcomes.

WLSP for a Changed World

This book and its necessity is premised, in part, on the idea that WLSP is vital to the well-being of our students and local and global communities in this new and changed world. Indeed, the 2020 pandemic made clear the relevance and value of WLSP for world language education and community engagement initiatives at institutions of higher learning. As the scholarship on world languages in the era of COVID-19 will most certainly show, the gap in organization and institution outreach, service, and assistance to immigrant and other underserved communities as a result of social distancing will more than likely be filled with the help of world language scholars and students with training and experience in WLSP. Using communication technology and social media platforms, these individuals possessed the specific language skills, cultural knowledge and sensibilities, professional skills, and empathy to provide compassionate care alongside community partners to those most affected, using the latest communication technology and social media platforms. Though this is a new and extreme challenge for humanity, it has opened our eyes to the potential and necessity of WLSP for our students and local and global communities.

In light of recent history, it is overdue for world language programs and institutions of higher education to reorient their priorities, values, and purpose. WLSP must be brought from the margins to the center of world language education alongside linguistics and literature and cultural studies. It is not enough to create undergraduate certificate programs in specific areas of WLSP. Master's- and PhD-level coursework in WLSP must follow in order to better equip our students to advance the field in its reach and impact. Graduating master's and PhD students with specializations in WLSP will make a real impact in this world through their scholarship and teaching, community engagement, service and outreach, and ways in which they approach and conduct their work and serve their communities. They will most certainly be among the first to provide the necessary support and assistance to immigrant and other underserved communities during times of crisis should the need arise.

For such a transformation in world language education to occur, it is necessary for language educators of all backgrounds to participate. As this book illustrates, you can begin to develop and integrate WLSP into your curricula even now, regardless of training, area of specialization, and experience in the professions. It is my hope that the strategies, teaching examples, and resources presented in the respective chapters will be of service in this endeavor. Keep in mind, however, that they are meant to be points of departure. How you adapt these ideas and transform them to suit your strengths, needs, perspective, and interests, as well as those of your students, institution, and local community, is up to you.

Appendix A

Selected Print and Online Resources

THE FOLLOWING PRESENTS A selected bibliography of print and online resources for teachers and students interested in teaching WLSP. Though many of the print sources are drawn from the literature on SSP, they nonetheless serve as a good basis from which to develop curriculum in WLSP no matter the target language. WLSP is a growing field, and research and online materials are increasing rapidly. As such, this list is intended to be neither exhaustive nor comprehensive. Also note that the links and online resources listed here are subject to change, given the rapidly changing nature of technology. The following list is thus offered with the intent of providing teachers and students with a point of departure for further inquiry.

Books, Manuals, and Edited Volumes

King de Ramírez, Carmen, and Barbara Lafford, eds. 2018. *Transferable Skills for the 21st Century: Preparing Students for the Workplace Through World Languages for Specific Purposes.* Provo: Sabio Books.

This edited volume provides world language educators with specific examples of how language and social skills taught through WLSP and CSL help prepare students for the modern workplace. Specific transferable skills identified as desirable by employers are highlighted in eight case studies that are divided into four main areas: critical thinking, adaptability, intercultural competence, and collaboration. Thoughtful in its approach and well organized by the editors, this book is a great resource for any world language educator interested in learning about the teaching of WLSP and how it is relevant for students, departments, the marketplace, and society today. It is also helpful in providing teachers useful pedagogical examples and tools for the teaching of WLSP.

Aguirre Beltrán, Blanca. 2012. *Aprendizaje y enseñanza de español con fines específicos: comunicación en ámbitos académicos y profesionales*. Alcobendas (Madrid): Sociedad General Española de Librería.

This book, written in Spanish and from the perspective of SSP in Spain, provides a foundation in WLSP teaching and learning. It covers foundational theoretical and methodological issues in both languages for academic and other specific purposes and includes models for the development of courses. This book is useful for educators interested in learning about how LSP, as a field and area of teaching, is conceptualized and approached in Spain.

Trace, Jonathan, Thom Hudson, and James Dean Brown, eds. 2015. *Developing Courses in Languages for Specific Purposes*. University of Hawai'i at Mānoa: National Foreign Language Resource Center. http://hdl.handle.net/10125/14573.

An online resource, this edited volume presents ten case studies in WLSP course design in the areas of languages for medical, business, and alternative purposes. Spanning a variety of world language areas, including Mandarin, Korean, Spanish, Russian, Arabic, and Hawaiian, the chapters serve as useful models for curriculum design. In addition, the introductory and concluding chapters help contextualize the field of WLSP and its current state as an area of world language education.

Lear, Darcy. 2019. *Integrating Career Preparation into Language Courses*. Washington, DC: Georgetown University Press.

This book provides practical ideas and strategies for preparing world language students for workplace success through the integration of WLSP. Concise, it consists of six chapters addressing different professional skills (e.g., gatekeeping, networking, and digital literacy), an annotated list of suggested readings, and an appendix with useful teaching resources, including assessment rubrics. Teachers of all languages and educational and professional backgrounds will find this book and its models useful in enhancing their current curriculum.

Sánchez-López, Lourdes, ed. 2013. *Scholarship and Teaching on Languages for Specific Purposes*. Birmingham: University of Alabama, UAB Digital Collections. http://contentdm.mhsl.uab.edu/cdm/compoundobject/collection/faculty/id/161/rec/1.

An online resource, this edited volume provides a comprehensive overview of trends in the research and teaching of WLSP. Consisting of twelve chapters, the book is organized into five sections addressing theoretical models, the current state of the field, WLSP programs and practices, teaching and learning experiences, and methodology. Teachers and administrators will find broad contextualization of the field and its issues, as well as specific program and teaching case studies designed for working through common issues in curriculum and program design.

Litzler, Mary Frances, Jesús García Laborda, and Cristina Tejedor Martínez, eds. 2016. *Beyond the Universe of Languages for Specific Purposes: The 21st Century Perspective*. Alcalá de Henares: Universidad de Alcalá.

This edited volume offers an overview of the field of WLSP from an international and interdisciplinary perspective. Ranging in language area and topic, the chapters are organized into three parts addressing teaching, business and marketing, and interpreting and translation in WLSP. The concepts, methods, and case studies presented in the respective chapters will be useful to world language educators.

Long, Mary K., ed. 2017. *Language for Specific Purposes: Trends in Curriculum Development*. Washington: Georgetown University Press.

This edited volume provides a comprehensive overview of the major issues and trends in the teaching of WLSP. Consisting of ten chapters spanning various language areas and WLSP topics, the book is organized into three main sections addressing new areas in WLSP curriculum development, instructor roles, and workplace realities through teaching. While the primary chapters provide teachers of any language useful case studies and models, the introductory chapters offer an overview of the current state of the field, including major trends and issues in curriculum development.

Journals and Special Editions

Global Business Languages

This journal includes research related to business languages in an international context. The articles present useful case studies that may be used as models for curriculum development in business languages.

Hispania 93, no. 1 (2010)

This special issue includes articles addressing CSL in the context of SSP. Educators of all language areas will find the case studies and issues addressed useful in developing curricula in WLSP and CSL. Given the historical significance of this issue, the articles are recommended as supplemental reading for any course or module on CSL in WLSP.

Journal of Languages for Specific Purposes (JLSP)

This journal presents research on WLSP from an interdisciplinary and international perspective. It includes useful case studies as well as articles addressing theoretical and methodological issues relevant to the teaching of WLSP. Articles are published in English, Spanish, German, French, and Italian.

Modern Language Journal 96, no. s1 (2012)

This special focus issue on language for specific purposes provides a good overview of the history and development of the field in the United States and globally, as well as key issues and trends in the research and teaching of WLSP. Many of the articles are considered important texts in WLSP scholarship, especially for their historical context, scope and vision, and inclusion of community service learning. As a result, this issue is highly recommended as a supplementary text for any foundational course in WLSP.

Revista de lenguas para fines específicos (RLFE)

This journal presents articles on WLSP from an international and interdisciplinary perspective. Among the articles, teachers will find useful case studies relating to different topics and language areas in WLSP, including on CSL. Though based in Spain, the journal publishes on WLSP research in any language area, and publications appear in various languages, including English, Spanish, French, and German.

Online Resources

American Council on the Teaching of Foreign Languages
(ACTFL; www.actfl.org)

In addition to current world language teaching standards and links to research, the ACTFL website includes a page dedicated to languages and careers (under Career Resources).

Centers for International Business Education and Research
(CIBER; www.ciberweb.msu.edu)

The CIBER website contains a wealth of information for world language educators especially interested in business languages, including information on current programs, research, CIBER institutions, business research and teaching awards, outreach and educational initiatives, and professional development workshops.

Network of Business Language Educators (NOBLE; www.nble.org)

Among the many resources included in the NOBLE website are links to and information on WLSP teaching resources, journals and research, program initiatives, conferences, and professional development workshops, webinars, and events.

National Council on Interpreting in Health Care (NCIHC; www.ncihc.org)

The NCIHC website provides useful information and links for teachers interested in integrating interpreting as a part of their WLSP lesson plan or course. Specifically, the site contains bibliographic resources on interpreting in health care and information on standards and ethics, interpreter qualifications, and workshops, as well as links to other useful websites, like the Cross Cultural Health Care Program.

American Translator's Association (ATA; www.atanet.org)

This website is useful in helping teachers interested in preparing students for careers as translators. The ATA site contains information on translator standards, resources, professional development opportunities, and the ATA certification process.

International Medical Interpreter Association (IMIA; www.imiaweb.org)

The IMIA website includes information on medical interpreting standards and interpretive service providers (ISP) certification as well as resources on medical terminology, alternative medicine, intercultural competence, health disparities, mental health, and other health, social, and cultural issues relevant to medical interpreting.

Cross Cultural Health Care Program (www.xculture.org)

This website contains resources on developing intercultural competence for medical interpreting, including information on workshops and trainings and links for professional development.

EthnoMed (www.ethnomed.org)

This website provides teachers with resources for developing cultural competence in medical interpreting and includes cultural information on different immigrant and refugee communities in the United States, topical clinical pamphlets translated in various languages, and links to other relevant websites.

Appendix B

Medical Spanish Course Syllabus and Calendar (Intermediate/Advanced Levels)

Course Description

Medical Spanish is a course that will help prepare students for the medical field in the twenty-first century. There are many places in the world where Spanish is spoken besides the United States, but the United States is especially important for the focus of this course considering our location in the world. The United States today is experiencing an influx of Latinx immigrants from South and Central America as well as the Caribbean. They bring with them not only their language but culture as well, including perceptions about medicine, health, and healing. This course will teach students not only about medical Spanish vocabulary and phrases but also about how language and culture impact perceptions and reception of health care as well as how health care is ensconced in culture, which impacts how health services are oriented toward the Latinx/Spanish-speaking community. Students will walk away from this course able to be interpreter-ready as well as interculturally sensitive and competent health care providers able to navigate the Spanish-English language and life worlds.

Course Learning Objectives (Using "Can-Do" Statements)
By the end of the course, students can . . .

- Direct language use toward the specific context of health and healing, including medical and other health and wellness occupational services.
- Direct appropriate cultural resources toward combatting unequal resources in the health care industry for the Latinx population in the United States.
- Direct appropriate cultural resources toward the implementation of health care services.
- Direct resources toward the betterment and well-being of communities of the target language, including Latinx and other non-English speaking immigrant communities in the United States.

Course Learning Goals (Using "Can-Do" Statements)

By the end of the course, students can . . .

- Speak Spanish in such a way as to provide adequate health and wellness services in service to the US Latinx population for the betterment of our local communities and the United States.
- Speak Spanish in such a way as to provide adequate and culturally sensitive care to patients and communities in need of medical and health and wellness services for the betterment of our local communities and the United States.
- Direct appropriate cultural resources toward the betterment of non-English speaking immigrant communities in favor of integrating within the United States and in favor of making the United States a better place for all.

Textbook

Chong, Nilda. 2002. *The Latino Patient: A Cultural Guide for Health Care Providers.* Yarmouth, ME: Intercultural Press.

Assignments

In-Class Assignments/Participation

- Students should do the assigned homework before coming to class. Class discussion and activities will be based on the work done at home. All class discussions and activities will be in Spanish, and students are expected to speak in the target language at all times. Class activities will include role-plays and workshops, and all students are expected to participate actively. Class attendance and participation are part of the final grade.

Homework Assignments

Homework will take on various formats, including written and oral practice. Class attendance is crucial to know what you will work on.

Reflection Journal

Students are to maintain a reflection journal over the course of the semester. The journals are intended to be a space for reflection on course content and discussions as they relate to student personal and professional experience and backgrounds. Writing prompts will be provided, and journal entries will be at least 250 words typed, though other forms of personal expression are welcome (subject to approval of the instructor). Journals will be collected twice during the semester, prior to the midterm and final.

Oral Presentations

Students will work in groups to present a topic selected. Students are expected to not only review vocabulary, but also to design and implement activities that promote the use of this vocabulary in an interactive way. Topics and groups will be assigned during the first week of class.

Calendar

- Week 1: Family Medicine
- Week 2: Cardiology
- Week 3: Emergency
- Week 4: Pediatrics
- Week 5: Gastroenterology
- Week 6: OB/GYN
- Week 7: Gerontology
- Week 8: Review; Midterm Exam
- Week 9: Otorhinolaryngology
- Week 10: Dermatology
- Week 11: Neurology
- Week 12: Ophthalmology
- Week 13: Urology
- Week 14: Immunology; Group Presentations
- Week 15: Pulmonology; Group Presentations
- Week 16: Final Exam

Appendix C

Lesson Plans in WLSP (Intermediate/Advanced Levels)

Lesson Plan Example 1: The Job Interview / Spanish for Commerce (Spanning 1 to 2 weeks)

Objectives
By the end of the class, students can . . .

- Identify appropriate and effective language for use in professional job application materials and interviews.
- Identify how culture informs appropriate and effective language use in a job application and hiring process.
- Reproduce a professional résumé and cover letter.
- Use language appropriately and effectively to talk about their background and professional skills in a mock job interview context.

Presentation/Discussion

- How many of you have had to apply for a job or do a job interview?
- What sorts of materials did you have to gather or put together to apply for the job?
- What sorts of information did you need to include in those job application materials? (Generate list of information with student input.)
- What sorts of questions were you asked during the interview? (Generate a list of questions with student input.)

Comprehension Activity (Material Culture and Audio-Visual)

- Present examples of calls for jobs, résumés, cover letters, and job interviews. Have students talk about the examples in groups of two or three. Have them generate a list of observations and develop strategies for writing a résumé and cover letter and for doing a job interview.

Reproduction Activity

- Option 1: Students compose a cover letter and résumé for a job chosen either by the teacher or by the students (in their area of specialty).
- Option 2: Students compose a script for a job interview and take turns interviewing one another.
- Option 3: Students compose job application materials in class for a job chosen by the teacher and prepare outside of class for a nonscripted mock interview with the teacher to be conducted during the next class period.

Reflection Activity (Written Assignment or In-Class Discussion)
"What role does language and culture play in the professional hiring process?"

- What decisions did you have to make with regard to register, vocabulary, grammar, body language, and so forth? What informed your decision-making?
- What did your background (identity, culture, cultural heritage, education, professional experience, etc.) and language skills contribute to your job application materials and interview? How did you incorporate them?
- What role did culture play in the interview process?
- How might knowledge about the culture of the country, professional field, workplace, and the interviewer themselves benefit you in the hiring process?

Lesson Plan Example 2: The Cardiovascular System / Spanish for Health Care

Objectives
By the end of class, students can . . .

- Identify vocabulary in the target language associated with the cardiovascular system.
- Reproduce a diagram of the cardiovascular system using vocabulary in the target language.
- Use the target language appropriately and effectively in discussing the cardiovascular system.
- Recognize the role that culture plays in understanding and approaching the heart and its relationship to health and wellness.

Presentation/Discussion Activity

- "The Two Fridas": Show image of the painting "The Two Fridas" by Frida Kahlo and generate vocabulary with students through the following discussion.
  - Do you know this woman? Why is she painting this? Why is she dressed in this way? Compare and contrast the images of the two Fridas. What do you notice about the heart? Why do you think the heart is drawn this way?
  - Show image of an actual bisected heart: How does it compare to this image of a real heart?

- Chapolin Colorado: Show image and symbol of Chapolin Colorado.
  - Here is a different depiction of a heart from Latin America. What do you notice about this superhero? What is the difference between this hero and Captain America? What do you think it means for Chapolin Colorado to have the heart as his emblem and shield? What sort of superhero do you think this is?
  - Show clip of Chapolin Colorado: What do you notice about this superhero (he's vulnerable, makes mistakes, etc.)? How does this representation of the heart compare and contrast with your own understanding of the heart and its association with emotions and personality qualities?

Input/Comprehension Activity

- Heart Diagram:
  - Have students draw a bisected heart and label the parts while generating the necessary vocabulary with the discussion below. (Note: accuracy in drawing is not important at this stage of the exercise; corrections will be made over the course of the lesson.)
  - Why did you draw your heart this way? What parts are necessary? What function do the pathways serve in the cardiovascular system? What function do the four chambers of the heart serve? What function do the lungs serve?
- The Cardiovascular System (a total physical response activity):
  - Have students reproduce the cardiovascular system by physically walking along the pathway of the heart, representing oxygen-poor blood entering the heart from the right atrium and ventricle and proceeding to the lungs via the pulmonary arteries and back to the left atrium and ventricle as oxygen-rich blood before exiting into the body via the aorta.
  - Note: This activity can be accomplished using a large heart diagram that can be placed on the floor (purchased or made by the teacher or students) or by using physical props representing the various parts of the heart and cardiovascular system.

Reproduction Activity

- Heart Diagram Revisited:
  - Have students return to their original drawing and make corrections (draw new one if necessary, with correct parts and labels).
  - A quiz based on this diagram and vocabulary may also be used either during the next class period, at the end of the unit, or even the end of class if an advanced language course.

Reflection Activity

- Reflect on culture and the relationship between the heart and health and wellness (journal or discussion activity, time permitting).
  - Have students compare what they learned about the heart with Frida's representation of the heart as well as their own initial drawing.

— How does Frida understand the heart and its relationship to health in her painting? What does your drawing tell you about your own understanding of this relationship? How does modern Western medicine treat the heart and its relationship to health and wellness?

— What sorts of health problems do we associate with the heart (biological and emotional)? Who do you see when you experience heart problems? Who do you see when you experience problems of the heart?

— What does our emotional health have to do with our heart, and what role might cultural differences in understanding the heart play in treating conditions involving the heart?

Homework

- Produce an interpreting dialogue.
  - Note that an example, template, and guide are provided and should be made available to students.
  - This homework assignment can be used across all the systems addressed in a medical language course.

Appendix D

Assignments (Intermediate/Advanced Levels)

Reflection Journal (Prompt Example for Spanish for Law Enforcement)

Guidelines
Journal entries are a space for critical reflection on course content and discussion as they relate to your personal and professional experience and background. Address the following prompts in your reflection. Entries should be between 250 and 500 words in length. Other forms of personal expression will likewise be considered when appropriate (see the instructor).

Prompt
For use following a lesson on history and demographics of Latinx immigration to the United States.

- The Latinx population in the United States represent a broad and diverse range of nations, ethnicities, and cultures that arrived during different periods of US history and laws regarding immigration. One thing all immigrants have in common, however, is a story of migration, which includes their reasons for leaving and their dreams and desires for a new life in a new land. Do you know the migration story of your family? If so, please share what you know and are able to. How do you connect with your family's story, if at all? (Note: if you are not comfortable sharing your story or are unable to do so, you may discuss how you relate to your cultural heritage and identity). Also, how does your or your family's immigration story relate to the experiences of other Latinx immigrants to the United States as addressed in class.

Interpreter Dialogue Assignment Example (Medical Spanish)

Medical Dialogue

Dialogue template SAMPLE

> Date:
>
> Your name: MARIA GONZALES
>
> Setting: Urgent Care, Adult hospital
>
> Participants: Nurse Jackie, patient, and interpreter
>
> Tarea number: 1-Chapter: Cardiovascular system

1. Objective: What is the goal of this dialogue? The goal is to find out if Señora López is at risk of a heart attack due to smoking and sedentarism.
2. Context: Describe the situation, setting of the dialogue (place, type of communication, anything that needs clarification). This happens at the Church Clinic and is simultaneous.
3. Include online completed work.
4. Use dialogue as you would actual speech. Remember it can be bilingual
5. Describe characters and intentions when necessary
6. Be creative!
7. Characters are: Mrs. Lopez, Nurse Jackie, and interpreter.
8. Character Description: La señora Lopez tiene 40 años y es de México, Jalisco, pero vive en Memphis. El Dr. Heart es de Nashville y es anglosajón, de orígenes alemanes y tiene 38 años. _____ es un/a intérprete medico que tomó la clase de medical Spanish con la profesora Ruggiero y ahora está estudiando medicina.
9. Preconference information: Nurse Jackie to interpreter: This patient is LEP (limited English proficiency) and needs your help as an interpreter. I have to assess what is wrong with her and we have to be quick, this is a triage.

I am *(your first name)*, your interpreter.	*Soy (tu nombre), tu intérprete.*
I will interpret everything you say in the first person and keep it all confidential.	*Voy a interpretar todo lo que diga en primera persona y será confidencial.*
Please speak to each other in short sentences, and I may interrupt for clarification.	*Por favor hable en oraciones cortas y quizás lo/la interrumpa por clarificación.*
Can I be your interpreter today?	*¿Puedo ser tu intérprete hoy?*

Your dialogue here:

Nurse/Enfermera: Jackie	Patient: Señora López
Enfermera (with a big smile): Good afternoon Mrs. Lopez! My name is Jackie and I will be your nurse today. This is _____ and they will be your medical interpreter for today.	
	Paciente (She is a bit confused and feels lost. She feels she is not dressed elegant enough to be at the doctor's office.): Está bien, gracias
Enfermera (in a nice calm tone, with all the patience in the world): What seems to be the problem today? How are you feeling?	
	Paciente (Now she is moving her hands a lot.): Bueno . . . estaba pintando mi casa y fumando un cigarrillo, y de repente mi corazón empezó a latir rápido y me caí . . . de una escalera y me golpeé la espalda y un poco la cabeza . . . me duele mucho el pecho.
Enfermera (looking surprised): Oh my goodness, Mrs. Lopez! How many cigarettes do you smoke a day? How long ago have you had this pain? Does anyone in your family have medical problems such as high blood pressure?	
	Paciente: Hace como una hora y sí, mis padres tienen la presión sanguínea alta. Y fumo 8 paquetes al día.
Enfermera: Have you ever had a heart attack?	
	Paciente: *respirando profundamente* No . . . puedo . . . respirar . . . *Señora Lopez se desmaya*
Ahora la paciente está en el piso, el interprete no sabe qué hacer, la enfermera está muy preocupada y transpira mucho, casi parece que llora.	
Enfermera: Code blue! Bring the doctor! Mrs. Lopez can you hear me?	
	Paciente: *todavia desmayada*
Enfermera: Mrs. Lopez you might be suffering from a heart attack or internal bleeding from your fall. We're going to take you down to get a CT scan.	
	Paciente: *todavia desmayada*
Enfermera: Let's go! Hurry!	

Composition Exercise Example (Cover Letter for Job Interview; Intermediate/Advanced Levels)

Job Posting Announcement

Guidelines
Write a cover letter for the following job posting. Use the examples discussed in class, the template provided, and online resources to help you compose your professional cover letter. Remember that the cover letter is your opportunity to make a good first impression, and in many cases it serves as the application itself. Be sure to address the specific points addressed in the job posting and to highlight how your education, training, professional experience, personal background, and language skills make you an outstanding candidate for this job.

Job Title: Senior Advisor, Multicultural Marketing (Prominent Research Hospital)

Job Description
Under the leadership of the Sr. Director of Multicultural Marketing and Business Development, the Sr. Advisor of Core Programs is responsible for supporting the multicultural strategic, operational, and functional activity needs of this organization's core programs, enterprise campaigns, and activities by integrating multiethnic insights, trends, and business intelligence across the enterprise to meet and exceed the organization's multicultural financial and brand awareness goals.

- Requires a customer-oriented individual, as well as detail-oriented, excellent organizational skills; speak and write in a clear and understandable manner for internal/external relations.
- Experience in business development and marketing to the Hispanic segment.
- Bilingual Spanish and English language required.
- Understands difficult verbal or written instructions, understand data processing applications.
- Must possess excellent diplomacy skills.
- Knowledge ordinarily acquired through bachelor's degree (master's degree a plus) and 8–10 years of experience in fundraising, marketing, business, or related field, including fundraising campaign segmentation, database management, strategic planning, and cost control. The Organization is an equal employment opportunity employer.

The Organization does not discriminate against any individual with regard to race, color, religion, sex, national origin, age, sexual orientation, gender identity, transgender status, disability, veteran status, genetic information, or other protected status.

Job Posting Announcement (Alternate Version)

Find a job posting in your preferred career path and write a cover letter for an application. Use the examples discussed in class, the template provided, and online resources to help you compose your cover letter. Remember that the cover letter is your opportunity to make a good first impression, and in many cases it serves as the application itself. Be sure to address the specific points addressed in the job posting and to highlight how your education, training, professional experience, personal background, and language skills make you an outstanding candidate for this job.

Appendix E

Assessments (Intermediate/Advanced Levels)

Exam (Language for Commerce)

Part I: Foundational (Short Written Questions Regarding Factual and Conceptual Knowledge)

- Types of questions: definition, identification, matching, fill-in-the-blank, comprehension
- Example: "Define the following terms: Cultural literacy, globalization, multinational corporation, economic risk, etc."

Part II: Integrative (Mastery of Concepts through Application in Comparative and Reflexive Questions)

- Types of questions: analytical and comparative short-answer/essay
- Example: "Briefly compare and contrast the economic stability and concerns of [one of the countries addressed in this course] with that of the United States."

Part III: Processual and Attitudinal (Problem Solving)

- Types of questions: problem/project-based experiential questions/tasks
- Example: "Apply the cultural competency knowledge and professional language skills learned thus far to write a start-up business proposal for funding. The business needs to address a specific need of the local community of the target language. Briefly explain the company, the need it fulfills, and how it seeks to fulfill that need. Be sure to identify a vision/mission for the company."

Part IV: Reflexive Short Essay

- Types of questions: essay
- Example: "How do international business relations between countries discussed thus far reflect the cultural values of the respective nations?"

Appendix F

CSL Exit Survey

Rate your level of agreement with the following statements:

The project met the learning objectives for the course.

I	2	3	4	5
strongly agree	agree	neutral	disagree	strongly disagree

The project met the objectives of the community partners.

I	2	3	4	5
strongly agree	agree	neutral	disagree	strongly disagree

The project met its intended goals and objectives (i.e., project products).

I	2	3	4	5
strongly agree	agree	neutral	disagree	strongly disagree

The project was successful in bridging the community and university/college.

I	2	3	4	5
strongly agree	agree	neutral	disagree	strongly disagree

The project helped bridge classroom learning with real-world experience.

I	2	3	4	5
strongly agree	agree	neutral	disagree	strongly disagree

The project provided preprofessional experience.

1	2	3	4	5
strongly agree	agree	neutral	disagree	strongly disagree

The project exposed me to people of different backgrounds.

1	2	3	4	5
strongly agree	agree	neutral	disagree	strongly disagree

The project helped raise my awareness of issues and needs in the local community.

1	2	3	4	5
strongly agree	agree	neutral	disagree	strongly disagree

The project helped raise my awareness of issues and needs in the professional context of the project.

1	2	3	4	5
strongly agree	agree	neutral	disagree	strongly disagree

The project raised my awareness of issues and needs in professional bilingual language development.

1	2	3	4	5
strongly agree	agree	neutral	disagree	strongly disagree

The project helped improve my professional language skills.

1	2	3	4	5
strongly agree	agree	neutral	disagree	strongly disagree

The project helped improve my ability to communicate appropriately and effectively with people of different backgrounds (e.g., cultural, racial, ethnic, linguistic).

1	2	3	4	5
strongly agree	agree	neutral	disagree	strongly disagree

Appendix G

Sample Lesson Plan, Reading Guide, and Journal Prompt (Non-WLSP Course; Intermediate/Advanced Levels)

Lesson Plan on Counseling and *Love in the Time of Cholera* (Advanced Literature Course)

A note on context: A complex tale of love, passion, and propriety, *Love in the Time of Cholera*, by Gabriel García Márquez, speaks to specific historical and cultural circumstances impacting the lives of Colombians and many other Latin Americans during the early twentieth century. As the title suggests, the tale takes place during a cholera epidemic in an unnamed coastal city of Colombia. It is set in a time that also coincides with a period of modernization and the establishment of modern science and the modern medical practice in Latin America. The story contrasts the modern sensibilities of the esteemed Dr. Juvenal Urbino with the emotional Fermina Daza and the passionate Florentino Ariza, Fermina's forbidden childhood love. The story is rich in metaphor and can be read and interpreted critically and for its historical and cultural significance in any number of ways. Given this fact, a teacher may choose to develop a lesson plan that focuses on the characters of Dr. Urbino, Fermina, and Florentino and that has students reflect on how the entangled lives, social status, and behavior of the characters speak to societal norms and expectations regarding love, gender roles, and perceptions of tradition and modernity in early twentieth-century Colombia and Latin America. One possible way WLSP might help deliver such a lesson is by using the areas of medicine, journalism, or counseling as vehicles for contextualizing and commenting on the story and its social and cultural lessons. The emphasis in this case would not be in teaching medical Spanish, journalism, or counseling, but on using those contexts as ways to engage students in critically exploring the literary work and time period and in building comparative bridges linking the book and its themes with other Latin American literary works of the same time period and with students' own understanding of the major themes and issues raised in the book. In this sample lesson plan, a role-play counseling scenario is the WLSP centerpiece that helps to deliver the lesson objectives.

Objectives

By the end of the lesson, students can . . .

- Identify and explain the key characters, relationship, and plot of *Love in the Time of Cholera*.
- Identify and use professions-specific language (focus: counseling) in discussing *Love in the Time of Cholera*.
- Explain historical and cultural significance of *Love in the Time of Cholera* in comparison with current social and cultural perspectives on relevant relationship issues.

Book Comprehension Check (Main Character and Plot Review)

Ask students comprehension questions in the target language based on the reading and reading guide completed for the present class (see Reading Guide).

Presentation/Discussion

- Have students generate vocabulary and phrases relating to relationships and relationship issues and introduce basic counseling vocabulary and phrases appropriate for role-play activity.
  - Where in the literature that we have read thus far or in popular culture and your own experience have you experienced similar relationship issues and drama?
  - What do you or the characters you're thinking about do when confronted with these issues? Is there anyone you go to talk to about relationships (friends, family, someone in the community, a professional)? When is it necessary to talk with a professional counselor? Do you think the characters in *Love in the Time of Cholera* could benefit from seeing a counselor?
- Briefly describe a typical counseling experience, introducing counseling vocabulary (e.g., attending phrases) along the way:
  - When I go to see a counselor . . .
  - Note: Basic attending skills focus on developing rapport and allowing "clients" to reflect on their own experiences for analysis in conversation with the therapist. If possible and available, play a brief example of a counseling session from a popular show or movie the students may be familiar with.

Role-Play Activity

Place students in groups of four. Ask them to develop open-ended questions in relation to the characters and situation in the text that allow for flow of conversation and for the "clients" to explore the emotions underlying the experience. Then ask them to write a script for a counseling scenario between the three characters using their questions. Time permitting, have them perform the scenarios. Alternately, and if they are more advanced students or native speakers, ask them to improvise the performance of the counseling scenario.

Follow up Discussion

Briefly have students reflect on how the complicated relationship between Dr. Urbino, Fermina, and Florentino speaks to broader cultural issues. Why, for instance, is Fermina's and Florentino's passion so problematic? How is Dr. Urbino's love for Fermina different? Is it any better? Why are these issues important in the context of the book and the time period in which it is set? How do we know this? What do the different characters represent? What is the message that the author is trying to convey with this love triangle?

Take-Home Assignment

Have students reflect on the broader implications of the central themes addressed in the lesson as they relate to modern-day Latin America and their own lives (see Journal Prompt).

Reading Guide: *Love in the Time of Cholera* (Focusing on Dr. Urbino, Fermina, and Florentino)

1. Who are Fermina and Florentino?
2. Describe the relationship between Fermina and Florentino.
3. Why are Fermina and Florentino unable to be together?
4. Who is Dr. Urbino?
5. Why does Fermina marry Dr. Urbino?
6. Describe the relationship between Dr. Urbino and Fermina.
7. What happens to Florentino during his time apart from Fermina?
8. What happens between Fermina and Florentino following Dr. Urbino's death?
9. What does the relationship between Dr. Urbino, Fermina, and Florentino have to do with the illness of cholera?
10. What are the major themes and issues raised in the book through the relationship of Dr. Urbino, Fermina, and Florentino?
11. How does the complicated relationship between the three characters relate to the broader social context of the book (early twentieth-century Colombia)?
12. How do the issues raised in the book relate to societal norms and expectations regarding love today (in Latin America, the United States, and globally)?

Journal Prompt

Write a brief 250–500-word journal entry based on the following prompt: Reflect on how the central themes and issues of *Love in the Time of Cholera* might be relevant to today's society (Latin America, the United States, and globally). Consider the themes of passion and propriety, gender roles and relationships, occupation and social status, societal norms and expectations, and tradition and modernity. How similar or different is our conception of love today? How do the characters and themes of *Love in the Time of Cholera* resonate with your own life and experience with love?

Appendix H

Interpreter Dialogue Template
(Intermediate/Advanced Levels)

FILL IN THE DIALOGUE boxes. If assigned as a homework or in-class written assignment, translate the dialogue from English to the target language and vice versa (see the following template). When used as a simultaneous interpreting exercise, ask students to write a dialogue of a service provider and client/patient without the corresponding translation. In other words, ask them to create a dialogue in the language of the respective speaker and then to interpret the text from English to the target language and from the target language to English.

Dialogue template

> Date:
>
> Your name:
>
> Participants:

Context

> Setting:
>
> Objective: What is the goal of this dialogue?
>
> Context: Describe the situation, setting of the dialogue (place, type of communication, anything that needs clarification).
>
> Characters:
>
> Character Description:
>
> Preconference information [if relevant]: [e.g., This client/patient is limited English proficiency (LEP).]

Note

> Write dialogue as you would actual speech.
>
> Remember that scripts can be bilingual [if relevant].
>
> Describe characters and intentions when necessary. Be creative!

Interpreter introductory statement [translate/state in the target language to client/ service provider prior to beginning dialogue]: I am *(your first name)*, an interpreter. I will interpret everything you say in the first person and keep it all confidential. Please speak to each other in short sentences, and I may interrupt for clarification. Can I be your interpreter today?

Write your dialogue here:

Service Provider	Client/Patient
[Insert service provider dialogue in English here.]	[Insert translation of service provider dialogue in the target language here for homework or in-class assignment; in simultaneous interpreting scenario, leave blank.]
[Insert translation of client/patient dialogue in English here for homework or in-class assignment; in simultaneous interpreting scenario, leave blank.]	[Insert client/patient dialogue in target language here.]
[Etc.]	
	[Etc.]

Appendix I

Community Engagement Lesson Plan and World Café (Intermediate/Advanced Levels)

Spanish for Community Engagement Lesson (Advanced Spanish Language Course)

Objectives
By the end of the class, students can . . .

- Identify appropriate and effective language for use in professional community organizing context.
- Identify how culture informs appropriate and effective language use in a community organizing context.
- Produce a community event or program that addresses the needs of the local community.
- Use language appropriately and effectively to talk about issues of relevance to the local community in the context of community organizing.

Presentation and Discussion
Present examples of local community centers and organizations and the services, programs, and events they organize to meet needs of the local community of the target language. Introduce relevant vocabulary and grammar in context. If possible, invite a guest from one of the community centers and organizations to discuss what they do.

Reproduction Activity
Ask students to generate a written proposal for an event or program that would address a current need of the local community in the target language. This project may be done as a class or in small groups. If done in small groups, it may be assigned as out-of-class work. Note that small groups also allow for in-class presentations. Ask the students to include the following in their proposal:

- What is the need being addressed by this proposed project?
- What is the proposed program or event?
- How will the event or program address the need?

World Café Activity

Topic: Community Organizing (Culture Focus)
Materials needed:

- Poster-size paper (four to five sheets, or one per group table)
- Pens, markers, pencils, etc.

Instructions

Divide class into four groups and designate a table leader for each group. Provide each group with poster-sized paper and writing utensils. Inform students that they may write and draw ideas and thoughts during discussion on the poster-sized paper. Also, inform table leaders that they will be responsible for sharing the ideas generated at their respective tables with the class at the end of the World Café discussion. Present one question at a time, allowing five minutes for each. At the end of each question, have all but the table leaders switch tables. Rather than rotate as a group, students should find a table with new participants for each question. When the questions are completed, ask table leaders to share the collective results of their respective table discussions with the rest of the class.

Questions

- What are the demographics of our local Latinx population? What cultures and languages are represented?
- What are the most pressing needs of the local Latinx and other immigrant populations in our community today?
- How are these needs informed by cultural similarities and differences among the Latinx population, but also between non-Latinx service providers and the Spanish-speaking communities they serve?
- How is knowledge of the Spanish language and culture useful in helping address the needs of local Spanish-speaking immigrants?

Appendix J

HL Interpreting, Cover Letter, and Résumé Activities (Intermediate/Advanced Levels)

Interpreting Activity

Objectives

- Resource HL cultural knowledge and language skills.
- Build intercultural competence through critical reflection.
- Empower HLs by placing them in a role model and mentorship position vis-à-vis peer L2 learners.

Instructions

Use the interpreting activity template and model introduced in chapter 8. Assign an interpreting dialogue to all students derived from the template and ask students to individually translate the text in the interpreter field (homework or in-class). Afterward (next class or same day), divide students into groups of three. Ideally, distribute HLs evenly among the groups in mixed L2 and HL classrooms. Follow the interpreting activity outlined in chapter 8, performing the interpreting scenario as per the script and later improvised among the class. For HLs specifically, emphasize fluency in conversation. In follow-up discussion, use HL variations in the interpretation to highlight to the class issues of linguistic and cultural diversity and fidelity of meaning in interpreting. Additionally, ask HLs to reflect, in journals or in class discussion, on their respective experiences with interpreting (informal and formal). Note that this may be a sensitive topic for some students. If this is the case, then a journal assignment may be the best alternative.

Questions

Consider the following with the students in follow-up discussion to interpreting activity:

- What differences are evident between the different interpreter translations (e.g., word choice, expressions, use of grammar, body language)?

- What role does culture, nationality, regionalism, and personal background play in these differences?
- To what extent do such differences factor in the fidelity of the translation and in the overall experience for service providers and clients or communities of the target language?
- How might this information be useful to interpreters?

Narrative Cover Letter and Résumé Activity: "Have You Ever Thought of Becoming a (_)?"

Objective
Empower HLs to reflect on the strengths and potential benefits of their respective cultural backgrounds and language abilities for the job market and community.

Instructions
This activity consists of three parts: (1) an introductory reflection on current cultural representations of the target language community in the career field, (2) a brief reflection writing or discussion assignment, and (3) a written résumé and cover letter.

Part 1: Introductory Reflection
Generate discussion on contemporary representations of the target language population in the professional field focused on in this lesson or course. Wherever and whenever possible, use examples from diverse texts found in popular culture (e.g., literature, film, the internet, music, news media). Consider the following questions:

- Is the target language population represented and to what extent and in what capacity?
- How is the target language population and its respective culture(s) represented or portrayed? What issues (e.g., stereotypes, problems, needs) are raised in these representations?
- To what extent do they represent the actual cultures, languages, history, and social and health issues and needs of the target language population today?

Part 2: Reflection Essay
Ask students to write a brief reflection essay on whether they see themselves as professionals in the field in question. Consider the following questions:

- Have you ever considered a career in this professional field? If so, in what role or capacity? If not, why not?
- What role do social, cultural, and family dynamics play in your decision and ability to pursue, or not pursue, this career path?
- What advantages and benefits for self, the profession, and society might there be for HLs to become involved in this professional field?

Part 3: Cover Letter and Résumé

Ask students to compose a narrative cover letter and résumé for a position in the field. Encourage HLs to leverage their cultural heritage and bilingual language skills as strengths for this position. Ask them to consider the following questions:

- What cultural knowledge and language skills do I possess and bring that may be considered an asset for this position and field?
- What benefits do my cultural heritage and identity have for the company/service provider/organization and community?

References

Abbott, Annie. 2009. *Comunidades: Más allá del aula*. New York: Pearson.

Abbott, Annie, and Darcy Lear. 2010. "The Connections Goal Area in Spanish Community Service Learning: Possibilities and Limitations." *Foreign Language Annals* 43, no. 2: 231–45. https://doi:10.1111/j.1944-9720.2010.01076.x.

Abbott, Annie, and Rejane Dias. 2018. "Community-Based Learning for Critical Career Exploration and Professional Skill Building." In *Transferable Skills for the 21st Century: Preparing Students for the Workplace through World Languages for Specific Purposes*, edited by Carmen King de Ramirez and Barbara Lafford, 37–63. Springville: Sabio Books.

Anderson, Neil J. 2002. *The Role of Metacognition in Second Language Teaching and Learning*. Washington, DC: Center for Applied Linguistics, ERIC Clearinghouse on Languages and Linguistics.

Angelelli, Claudia V. 2004. *Medical Interpreting and Cross-Cultural Interpreting*. New York: Cambridge University Press.

Barreneche, Gabriel Ignacio, and Héctor Ramos-Flores. 2013. "Integrated or Isolated Experiences? Considering the Case for Service-Learning in the Spanish Language Curriculum." *Hispania* 96, no. 2: 215–228.

Beaudrie, Sara M., Cynthia Ducar, and Kim Potowski, eds. 2014. *Heritage Language Teaching: Research and Practice*. New York: McGraw Hill.

Beaudrie, Sara. M., and Marta Fairclough. 2012. "Introduction: Spanish as a Heritage Language in the United States." In *Spanish as a Heritage Language in the United States: The State of the Field*, edited by Sara Beaudrie and Marta Fairclough, 1–17. Washington, DC: Georgetown University Press.

———, eds. 2012. *Spanish as a Heritage Language in the United States: The State of the Field*. Washington, DC: Georgetown University Press.

Bennett, Milton J. 1993. "Towards Ethnorelativism: A Developmental Model of Intercultural Sensitivity." In *Education for the Intercultural Experience*, 2nd ed., edited by R. Michael Paige, 21–71. Yarmouth: Intercultural Press.

Blanca, Aguirre Beltrán. 2012. *Aprendizaje y enseñanza de español con fines específicos: comunicación en ámbitos académicos y profesionales*. Alcobendas: Sociedad General Española de Librería.

Bloom, Melanie. 2008. "From the Classroom to the Community: Building Cultural Awareness in First Semester Spanish." *Language, Culture, and Language Curriculum* 21, no. 2: 103–19.

Brown, H. Douglas. 2000. *Principles of Language Learning and Teaching*. White Plains: Longman.

Byram, Michael. 1997. *Teaching and Assessing Intercultural Communicative Competence*. Multilingual Matters.

Byram, Michael, and Anwei Feng. 2004. "Culture and Language Learning: Teaching, Research, and Scholarship." *Language Teaching* 37, no. 3: 149–68.

Carreira, Maria, and Kagan, Olga. 2011. "The Results of the National Heritage Language Survey: Implications for Teaching, Curriculum Design, and Professional Development." *Foreign Language Annals* 44, no. 1: 40–64.

Clayton, Patti, Robert Bringle, and Julie Hatcher, eds. 2013. *Research on Service Learning: Conceptual Frameworks and Assessment*. Sterling: Stylus Publishing, LLC.

Dantas-Whitney, Maria. 2002. "Critical Reflection in Second Language Classroom through Audiotaped Journals." *System* 30: 543–555.

Deardorff, Darla K. 2006. "Identification and Assessment of Intercultural Competence as a Student Outcome of Internationalization." *Journal Studies in International Education* 10, no. 3: 241–66.

———. 2009. "Implementing Intercultural Competence Assessment." In *The Sage Handbook of Intercultural Competence*, edited by Darla K. Deardorff, 477–91. Thousand Oaks: Sage Publications.

Derby, LeAnn, Jean W. LeLoup, James Rasmussen, and Ismênia Sales de Souza. 2017. "Developing Intercultural Competence and Leadership through LSP Curricula." In *Language for Specific Purposes: Trends in Curriculum Development*, edited by Mary Long, 73–86. Washington, DC: Georgetown University Press.

Dewey, John, and Albion W. Small. 1897. *My Pedagogic Creed*. New York: E. L. Kellogg & Co.

Doyle, Michael. 2018. "Spanish for the Professions and Specific Purposes: Curricular Mainstay." *Hispania* 100, no. 5: 95–101.

Drugan, Joanna. 2017. "Ethics and Social Responsibility in Practice: Interpreters and Translators Engaging With and Beyond the Professions." *The Translator* 23, no. 2: 126–142.

Falce-Robinson, Juliet, and Darci Strother. 2012. "Language Proficiency and Civic Engagement: The Incorporation of Meaningful Service-Learning Projects in Spanish Language Courses." *Interdisciplinary Humanities* 29, no. 3: 73–87.

Fink, Dee L. 2003. *Creating Significant Learning Experiences: An Integrated Approach to Designing College Courses*. San Francisco: Jossey-Bass.

Freire, Paolo. 2006. *Pedagogy of the Oppressed*. Translated by M. B. Ramos. New York: Continuum.

Gibbons, Pauline. 2002. *Scaffolding Language, Scaffolding Learning: Teaching Second Language Learners in the Mainstream Classroom*. Portsmouth: Heinemann.

Grosse, Christine Uber, and Geoffrey Voght. 1990. "Foreign Language for Business and the Professions at US Colleges and Universities." *Modern Language Journal* 74, no. 1: 36–47.

Gurung, Regan A. R. 2014. *Multicultural Approaches to Health and Wellness in America*. Santa Barbara: ABC-CLIO.

Haukås, Åsta. 2018. *Metacognition in Language Learning and Teaching*. New York: Routledge.

Hellebrandt, Josef, and Lucia T. Varona. 1999. *Construyendo Puentes (Building Bridges): Concepts and Models of Service-Learning in Spanish*. Washington, DC: American Association for Higher Education.

Isabelli, Casilde, and Stacey Muse. 2016. "Service-Learning in the Latino Community: The Impact on Spanish Heritage Language Students and the Community." *Heritage Language Journal* 13, no. 3: 331–53.

Joralemon, Donald. 2017. *Exploring Medical Anthropology*. New York: Routledge.

Julseth, David C. 2004. "The Hispanic Achievers Program: An Interdisciplinary Model for Service-Learning." In *Juntos: Community Partnerships in Spanish and Portuguese*, edited by Josef Hellebrandt, Jonathan Arries, Lucia Verona, and Carol Klein, 140–153. Boston: Thomas/Heinle.

Kim, Deoksoon. 2020. "Learning Language, Learning Culture: Teaching Language to the Whole Student." *ECNU Review of Education* 3, no. 3: 519–41.

King de Ramírez, Carmen. 2016. "Creating Campus Communities for Latin@s Through Service-Learning: Heritage Learners' Broadcast University Spanish-Language Radio." *Heritage Language Journal* 13, no. 3: 382–404.

———. 2017. "Preparing Students for the Workplace: Heritage Learners' Experiences in Professional Community Internships." In *Language for Specific Purposes: Trends in Curriculum Development*, edited by Mary Long, 55–71. Washington, DC: Georgetown University Press.

King de Ramírez, Carmen, and Barbara Lafford. 2013. "Spanish for the Professions Program Design and Assessment." In *Scholarship and Teaching on Languages for Specific Purposes*, edited by Lourdes Sánchez-López. Birmingham: University of Alabama, UAB Digital Collections. http://contentdm.mhsl.uab.edu/cdm/compoundobject/collection/faculty/id/161/rec/19.

———. 2018. "Introduction." In *Transferable Skills for the 21st Century: Preparing Students for the Workplace through World Languages for Specific Purposes*, edited by Carmen King de Ramírez and Barbara Lafford, 21–36. Springville: Sabio Books.

———, eds. 2018. *Transferable Skills for the 21st Century: Preparing Students for the Workplace Through World Languages for Specific Purposes*. Provo: Sabio Books.

Knapp, Mark L., Judith A. Hall, and Terrence G. Horgan. 2014. *Nonverbal Communication in Human Interaction*. Boston: Wadsworth Cengage Learning.

Kramsch, Claire. 1998. *Language and Culture*. Oxford University Press.

Lafford, Barbara. 2012. "The Evolution of Languages for Specific Purposes: Update on Grosse and Voght (1991) in a Global Context." *Modern Language Journal* 96, no. s1: 1–27.

———. 2013. "The Next Frontier: A Research Agenda for Exploring Experiential Language Learning in International and Domestic Contexts." In *Selected Proceedings of the 16th Hispanic Linguistics Symposium*, edited by Jennifer Cabrelli Amaro, Gillian Lord, Ana de Prada Pérez, and Jessi Elana Aaron, 80–102. Somerville: Cascadilla Proceedings Project.

Lafford, Barbara, Annie Abbott, and Darcy Lear. 2014. "Spanish in the Professions and in the Community in the U.S." *Journal of Spanish Language Teaching* 1, no. 2: 171–86.

Lear, Darcy. 2012. "Language for Specific Purposes Curriculum Creation and Implementation in Service to the U.S. Community." *The Modern Language Journal* 96, no. s1: 158–72.

Lear, Darcy. 2019. *Integrating Career Preparation into Language Courses*. Washington, DC: Georgetown University Press.

Lear, Darcy, and Annie Abbott. 2009. "Aligning Expectations for Mutually Beneficial Community Service-Learning: The Case of Spanish Language Proficiency, Cultural Knowledge, and Professional Skills." *Hispania* 92, no. 2: 312–23.

Leeman, Jennifer. 2012. "Investigating Language Ideologies in Spanish as a Heritage Language." In *Spanish as a Heritage Language in the United States: The State of the Field*, edited by Sara Beaudrie and Marta Fairclough, 43–60. Washington, DC: Georgetown University Press.

Litzler, Mary Frances, Jesús García Laborda, and Cristina Tejedor Martínez, eds. 2016. *Beyond the Universe of Languages for Specific Purposes: The 21st Century Perspective*. Alcalá de Henares: Universidad de Alcalá.

Llombart-Huesca, Amália, and Alejandra Pulido. 2017. "Who Needs Linguistics? Service-Learning and Linguistics for Spanish Heritage Language Learners." *Hispania* 100, no. 3: 348–60.

Long, Mary K. 2010. "Spanish for the Professions Degree Programs in the United States: History and Current Practice." In *How Globalizing Professions Deal with National Languages: Studies in Cultural Studies and Cooperation*, edited by Michel Gueldry. Lewiston: Edwin Mellen Press.

———. 2017a. "Introduction: WLSP Studies and the Creation of Translingual and Transcultural Competence." In *Languages for Specific Purposes: Trends in Curriculum Development*, edited by Mary K. Long, 1–11. Washington, DC: Georgetown University Press.

———, ed. 2017b. *Language for Specific Purposes: Trends in Curriculum Development*. Washington, DC: Georgetown University Press.

Long, Sherri S., Jean W. LeLoup, LeAnn Derby, and Ramsamooj J. Reyes. 2014. "Fusing Language Learning and Leadership Development: Initial Approaches and Strategies." In *Dimension 2014: Uniting the Corps: Uniting the Core*, edited by Kristin Hoyt and Pete Swanson. Valdosta: Southern Conference on Language Teaching.

Luo Han, Yu Li, and Ming-Ying Li. 2019. "Heritage Learner Education in the United States: A National Survey of College-Level Chinese Language Programs." *Foreign Language Annals* 52, no. 1: 101–20.

Martínez, Glenn. 2010. "Medical Spanish for Heritage Learners: A Prescription to Improve the Health of Spanish-Speaking Communities." In *Building Communities, Making Connections*, edited by Susana Rivera-Mills and Juan Antonio Trujillo, 2–15. Newcastle upon Tyne: Cambridge Scholars Pub.

Martínez, Glenn, and Adam Schwartz. 2012. "Elevating 'Low' Language for High Stakes: A Case for Critical, Community-Based Learning in a Medical Spanish for Heritage Learners Program." *Heritage Language Journal* 9, no. 2: 37–49.

McBride, Kara. 2010. "Reciprocity in Service-Learning: Intercultural Competence Through SLA Studies." In *Proceedings of Intercultural Competence Conference*, edited by Beatrice Dupuy and Linda Waugh, 235–61. Tucson: Center for Education Resources in Culture, Language, and Literacy.

Medina, Almitra, and Leslie Gordon. 2014. "Service Learning, Phonemic Perception, and Learner Motivation: A Quantitative Study." *Foreign Language Annals* 47, no. 2: 357–71.

MLA (Modern Language Association). 2007. "Foreign Languages and Higher Education: New Structures for a Changed World." www.mla.org/pdf/forlang_news_pdf.pdf.

Nelson, Ardies, and Jessica Scott. 2008. "Applied Spanish in the University Curriculum: A Successful Model for Community-Based Service Learning." *Hispania* 91, no. 2: 446–60.

Penman, Christine. 2005. *Holistic Approaches to Language Learning.* Frankfurt am Main: P. Lang.

Pereira, Kelly Lowther. 2015. "Developing Critical Language Awareness via Service-Learning for Spanish Heritage Speakers." *Heritage Language Journal* 12, no. 2: 159–85.

Petrov, Lisa Amor 2013. "A Pilot Study of Service-Learning in a Spanish Heritage Speaker Course: Community Engagement Identity and Language in the Chicago Area." *Hispania* 96, no. 2: 310–27.

Reynolds, Rachel R. 2005. "Immigration Geographies, Multilingual Immigrants, and the Transmission of Minority Languages: Evidence from the Ibo Brain Drain." In *Language in Use: Cognitive and Discourse Perspectives on Language and Language Learning,* edited by Andrea Tyler, Mari Takada, Yiyoung Kim, and Diana Marinova, 214–23. Washington, DC: Georgetown University Press.

Risner, Mary. n.d. *Connecting World Language Curriculum to Workplace Skills.* Network of Business Language Educators (NOBLE). http://nble.org/ebook/.

Ruggiero, Diana. 2015. "Graduate Courses in Languages for Specific Purposes: Needs, Challenges, and Models." *Global Business Languages* 19, no. 5: 55–69. http://docs.lib.purdue.edu/gbl/vol19/iss1/5/.

———. 2016. "The Creating Communities, Engaged Scholarship Project (CruCES): Findings of a Study on Intercultural Sensitivity and Community Service Learning." In *Beyond the Universe of Languages for Specific Purposes,* edited by Mary Frances Litzler, Jesús García Laborda, and Cristina Tejedor Martínez, 59–64. Alcalá de Henares: Universidad de Alcalá.

———. 2017a. "Body Language Awareness: Teaching Medical Spanish Interpreting." In *Translation, Globalization and Translocation: The Classroom and Beyond,* edited by Concepcion Godeva, 185–206. New York: Palgrave Macmillan.

———. 2017b. "Community Service Learning, *Learning by Design,* and Heritage Learners: A Case Study." In *Multiliteracies Pedagogy and Language Learning: Teaching Spanish to Heritage Speakers,* edited by Gabriela Zapata and Manel Lacorte, 129–47. New York: Palgrave MacMillan.

———. 2017c. "The CruCES Project: A Consideration of Service Learning and Intercultural Sensitivity Among Heritage Learners." *Revista de Lenguas para Fines Específicos (LFE)* 23, no. 1: 45–62.

———. 2018a. "Lessons from the CruCES Project: Community Service Learning and Intercultural Sensitivity in the Foreign Language Classroom." In *AAUSC 2017 Volume: Engaging the World: Social Pedagogies and Language Learning,* edited by Stacey K. Bourns et al., 64–86. Boston: Cengage Learning.

———. 2018b. "Toward an Integrated Curriculum: Progress and Challenges in the Integration of Languages for Specific Purposes (LSP) and Community Service Learning in Foreign Language Programs after 2007." *ADFL Bulletin* 44, no. 2: 121–24.

———. 2018c. "Toward Collaborative, Equitable, and Sustainable Community Service Learning Projects in Languages for Specific Purposes." In *Languages for Specific Purposes: Curriculum Design and Community-Based Applications,* edited by Carmen King de Ramirez and Barbara Lafford, 259–86. Springville: Sabio Books.

———. 2019a. "A Significant Learning Approach to WLSP and Its Impact on Student Perceptions of the Field and its Definition." *Cuadernos de ALDEUU* 33: 21–52.

———. 2019b. "Toward a Framework for Heritage Learner Service Learning in Languages for Specific Purposes." *Revista Signos* 52, no. 101: 931–49.

Ruggiero, Diana, and Sean Hill. 2016. "New Trends in 21st Century Civic Engagement and Foreign Languages: Technology, Translation, and Social Justice." *Journal of Languages for Specific Purposes (JLSP),* no. 3 (March 2016): 51–62.

Sánchez-López, Lourdes. 2013a. "Introduction." In *Scholarship and Teaching on Languages for Specific Purposes,* edited by Lourdes Sánchez-López. Birmingham: University of Alabama, UAB Digital Collections. http://contentdm.mhsl.uab.edu/cdm/compoundobject/collection/faculty/id/161/rec/19.

———, ed. 2013b. *Scholarship and Teaching on Languages for Specific Purposes.* Birmingham: University of Alabama, UAB Digital Collections. http://contentdm.mhsl.uab.edu/cdm/compoundobject/collection/faculty/id/161/rec/19.

———. 2013c. "Service-Learning Course Design for Languages for Specific Purposes Programs." *Hispania* 96, no. 2: 383–96.

Sánchez-López, Lourdes, Mary Long, and Barbara Lafford. 2017. "New Directions in LSP Research in US Higher Education." In *Languages for Specific Purposes: Trends in Curriculum Development*, edited by Mary K. Long, 13–34. Washington, DC: Georgetown University Press.

Santiago-Rivera, Azara L., Patricia Arredondo, and Maritza Gallardo-Cooper. 2002. *Counseling Latinos and La Familia: A Practical Guide.* Thousand Oaks: Sage Publications.

Spitzberg, Brian H., and Gabrielle Changnon. 2009. "Conceptualizing Intercultural Competence." In *The Sage Handbook of Intercultural Competence*, edited by Darla K. Deardorff, 2–52. Thousand Oaks: Sage Publications.

Tocaimaza-Hatch, C. Cecilia, and Laura C. Walls. 2016. "Service-Learning as a Means of Vocabulary Learning for Second Language and Heritage Language Learners of Spanish." *Hispania* 99, no. 4: 650–65.

Trace, Jonathan, Thom Hudson, and James Dean Brown, eds. 2015. *Developing Courses in Languages for Specific Purposes.* University of Hawai'i at Mānoa: National Foreign Language Resource Center. https://scholarspace.manoa.hawaii.edu/bitstream/10125/14573/5/NW69.pdf.

Winkelman, Michael. 2009. *Culture and Health: Applying Medical Anthropology.* San Francisco: Jossey-Bass.

Wong, Ka F., and Yang Xiao. 2010. "Diversity and Difference: Identity Issues of Chinese Heritage Language Learners from Dialect Backgrounds." *Heritage Language Journal* 7, no. 2: 153–87.

Wu, Ming-Hsuan, Kathy Lee, and Genevieve Leung. 2014. "Heritage Language Education Investment among Asian American Middle Schoolers: Insights from a Charter School." *Language and Education* 28, no. 1: 19–33.

Zapata, Gabriela. 2011. "The Effects of Community Service Learning Projects on L2 Learners' Cultural Understanding." *Hispania* 94, no. 1: 86–102.

———. 2018. "A Match Made in Heaven: An Introduction to *Learning by Design* and its Role in Heritage Language Education." In *Multiliteracies Pedagogy and Language Learning: Teaching Spanish to Heritage Speakers*, edited by Gabriela C. Zapata and Manel Lacorte, 1–26. New York: Palgrave Macmillan.

Zapata, Gabriela, and Manuel Lacorte. 2018a. "A Match Made in Heaven: An Introduction to *Learning by Design* and Its Role in Heritage Language Education." In *Multiliteracies Pedagogy and Language Learning: Teaching Spanish to Heritage Speakers*, edited by Gabriela Zapata and Manel Lacorte, 1–26. New York: Palgrave MacMillan.

———, eds. 2018b. *Multiliteracies Pedagogy and Language Learning: Teaching Spanish to Heritage Speakers.* New York: Palgrave MacMillan.

About the Author

Diana Ruggiero is an associate professor of Spanish at the University of Memphis. She currently develops curricula in and researches world languages for specific purposes (WLSP) and community service learning (CSL), for which she is recognized nationally and internationally. A recipient of two national teaching awards from the American Council on the Teaching of Foreign Languages and American Association of Teachers of Spanish and Portuguese, her publications on WLSP and CSL appear in numerous peer-reviewed journals and edited volumes on Spanish for specific purposes and WLSP. In addition to giving invited conference presentations around the world on her research, Dr. Ruggiero frequently presents, gives workshops, and consults on WLSP teaching and curricula development for colleagues in world language higher education worldwide. In her spare time, she enjoys teaching aqua fitness as well as Latin dancing and cooking.

Index